SACRED
GEOGRAPHY

SACRED GEOGRAPHY

DECIPHERING HIDDEN CODES IN THE LANDSCAPE

Paul Devereux

Dedicated to the memory of John Michell (1933–2009)

Author's note

The material in this book has been culled from decades of my
own and others' fieldwork and literature research regarding ancient
sites and landscapes, but this has always been relatively fragmented in
the broader sense. This book presents what I think is the first 'joined-
up' look at the ancient phenomenon of sacred geography as a whole,
in all its main forms. Naturally, to explore every single facet of the topic
would take a whole series of volumes, but a broad swathe of types and
examples of sacred geography are covered in the following pages. I
have made a point of including some lesser-known examples and of
introducing recent and unfamiliar approaches to the subject area, such
as soundscapes and even gardens. They all speak of the ingenious ways
in which societies have projected their cultural maps and inner visions
onto the physical world. I hope readers will enjoy this journey through
some unusual and remarkable scenery.

All imperial–metric conversions are approximate.

An Hachette UK Company
www.hachette.co.uk

First published in Great Britain in 2010 by
Gaia, a division of Octopus Publishing Group Ltd
Endeavour House
189 Shaftesbury Avenue
London WC2H 8JY
www.octopusbooks.co.uk
www.octopusbooksusa.com

Distributed in the U.S. and Canada by Octopus Books USA:
c/o Hachette Book Group
237 Park Avenue
New York, NY 10017

ISBN 978-1-856-75322-7

A CIP catalogue record for this book is available from the British
Library.

Printed and bound in China
10 9 8 7 6 5 4 3 2 1

Contents

INTRODUCTION
Mindscapes, the varieties of sacred geography

Sacred geography is where the physical world and the 'otherworlds' of spirit or mind meet. Ancient and traditional peoples have found many different ways to invest their home territories with meaning, as this book illustrates.

A prime example is given by the *mamas* or religious elite of the Kogi Indians of northern Columbia, who are trained to see simultaneously both the physical world and the spirit otherworld, which they call *aluna*.[1] An infant who shows signs of having the potential to be a *mama* is raised in the deep darkness of caves, tended by elders and taught the way of the *mamas*. The child never sees daylight during this long period of sequestration, but in the course of training is taken out at night wearing a broad-brimmed hat, so as to see the landscape bathed in moonlight, yet not see the moon directly. After several years the child typically begins to rock back and forth and sing weird, otherworldly songs, and this is taken as a sign that it is time to lead the child – the initiate, in fact – out into the sunlight. The searing blast of daylight powers into the initiate's dreamy eyes, and from that moment on he can see both the physical terrain and *aluna* intermingled.

Ancient stone roads built by the Tairona people, the ancestral predecessors of the Kogi, traverse Kogi territory and have a special, spiritual meaning – they are intended to be walked as a religious exercise as well as used for mundane purposes. These physical roads are but the material traces of routes in *aluna*, and a *mama* can see them continuing on in that otherworld beyond their physical endpoints. A tall stone stands at the entrance to one of the old, abandoned Tairona towns and is criss-crossed with lines: this is the Map Stone, which marks both the physical and the otherworldly courses of the roads.

This is just one example of sacred geography. Such geographies of the soul may be small and intimate or cover large tracts of ground; they may be natural or constructed, or a combination of both. In the following chapters we will encounter examples of them all.

Cultural mindscapes

We will see that a basic way in which tribes and societies tried to sanctify their environment was by identifying natural landscape features as holy. These places became venerated – they were the first temples, found rather than built by human hand. The land became a repository for the tribal myths. It became sacred text.

Over time, following humanity's innate tendency to 'improve on nature', these places were subtly embellished, and then more boldly modified, until eventually

ABOVE A small figurine depicting a *mama*, a member of the religious elite of the Kogi Indians. The figure is capped with ornamental birds, which symbolize the magic capacities of the *mamas*.

entirely artificial features were created – monuments and temples. Whole landscapes were inscribed with strange patterns, images and otherworldly pathways, like the Kogi example. Physical and virtual geographies were superimposed on the material topography, ranging from virtual world centres to both visible and invisible routes for spirits to travel along. Special, choreographed routes were also devised for pilgrimages to the sacred places, whether natural or built. Constructed temples and monuments were on occasion arranged so as to relate to one another in a given landscape, or to acknowledge a natural, revered feature. Sometimes sacred geographies involved the creation of alignments to the movements of heavenly bodies, especially the sun and moon, so that landscapes merged with skyscapes, bringing heaven down to earth. Even gardens were created to express miniature mindscapes, to distil the sacred geography in which a culture felt itself to be living.

ABOVE **Ancient stone roads built by the ancestral predecessors of the Kogi, are intended to be walked as a religious exercise. This Map Stone stands outside the ruins of an old Tairona settlement and is criss-crossed with lines which mark both the physical and the otherworldly courses of the roads.**

directions and plunging their bare arms into the water to feel ocean currents playing on their skin. And we should guard against thinking that such mindscapes were for purely utilitarian purposes, for in ancient times pragmatic activities such as hunting and fishing also had spiritual dimensions. As one observer has pointed out, the Pacific islanders' mapping systems were also used for 'the storage and retrieval of other kinds of cultural information – myths, spells, ceremonies, chants, recitations, etc.'[3]

Now archeologists and anthropologists are increasingly coming to appreciate that probably the most usual type of non-visual sensory mapping was the use of sound. Echoes, whispering or burbling waters, musical rocks (lithophones), soughing wind and other acoustic phenomena were often considered to signal the presence of gods and spirits of various kinds, and this all helped to delineate the contours of ancient sacred geographies.

Such a mythic and sensory relationship with the environment was given the term 'participation mystique' by the anthropologist Lucien Lévy-Bruhl,[4] by which he meant a local relationship with the land that went beyond mere utility and subsistence. Another anthropologist, A. P. Elkin, put it well when writing about indigenous Australasian peoples: 'The bond between a person and his (or her) country is not merely geographical or fortuitous, but living and spiritual and sacred. His country ... is the symbol of, and gateway to, the great unseen world of heroes, ancestors and life-giving powers which avail for man and nature.'[5]

In the West, this kind of relationship was noted at least as long ago as ancient Greece, where there were two words for subtly different senses of place, *chora* and *topos*. *Chora* is the older of the two terms and was a holistic reference to place: place as expressive, place as a keeper of memory, and mythic presence. *Topos*, on the other

Sensory and mythic relationships with the environment

Not all sacred geographies relied on either bodily or mental eyes – some were sensory in other ways. For instance, a beach near Sawaieke on the Pacific island of Fiji is believed by traditional Fijians to be the haunt of ancestral spirits, on account of the vanilla-like scent of the sands there.[2] Even touch could be used as an element in constructing a cultural mindscape, as South Pacific islanders have demonstrated. They could – and still can – navigate the waters of their archipelagos by combining myth, astronomy, bird flight, knowledge of wind hand, signified place in much the way we think of it nowadays – simple location, and the objective, physical features of a locale, or topography. Ultimately, even sacred places became *topoi* as Western culture developed.

There are implications to mythic mapping that we usually fail to appreciate. If a tribal or traditional society is removed from its native territory, which reinforces cultural identity and a sense of belonging by encoding the tribe's collective memory in the form of its myths and legends, or if such a landscape is destroyed or radically altered, then it can cause a people's collective soul to die, leading to social decay.

Mapping worldviews

We may smile slightly condescendingly at these ancient and traditional ways of mapping the world, yet while we consider our modern maps as representing the world-as-it-really-is, we forget that there are no maps of the world, only maps of worldviews. This holds true for us as much as for any tribe or society that has gone before. Indeed, our modern maps are superimposed with various kinds of imaginary features, such as grids of lines, demarcations of tropical zones, international date lines, a variety of place symbols, different scales, and so on. There used to be a somewhat weak classroom joke that the equator is a menagerie lion that runs around the middle of the earth – a reference to it being an imaginary line running across the centre of world maps. Lewis Carroll used jest to make the same point: in his *Sylvie and Bruno Concluded*, where we learn of a map with a scale of 'a mile to the mile', which 'has never been spread out yet', and in his *The Hunting of the Snark* with the Bellman's blank map of the ocean – a map that the whole crew could understand because it was bereft of 'conventional signs'.

Our present worldview increasingly sees the land in terms of economic and social utility. Expressive qualities of place are remorselessly marginalized. Topography has replaced chorography. We are only just beginning to wrestle with the implications of this.

Being here

How a culture maps its world says much about its way of thinking about its environment, about how its soul and the soul of the world, the *anima mundi*, interact. In today's modern world we are increasingly moving our viewpoint 'off Earth', with satellite navigation devices in our cars divorcing us from the actual experience of travelling through the landscape; we use geodetic positioning-system instruments; we walk with cellphones or recording devices stuck to our ears so that we are hardly aware of where we are. Despite all the technological precision, we are losing ourselves because we are no longer here. It is perhaps timely to reacquaint ourselves with other, more psychologically wholesome ways of being on this planet.

BELOW Modern maps show date lines, scale and political boundaries, which indicate that modern cultures view the world in physical terms. Ancient and traditional cultures viewed their world very differently.

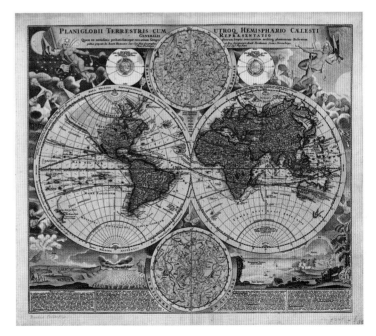

THE TOPOGRAPHY OF MYTH

Venerated Natural Places

*I*t was the land itself that first whispered the idea of the holy to humanity, and the earliest sacred geographies or mindscapes were mapped on unaltered natural landscapes. People venerated specific topographical features because they were considered to be the homes of mythic beings – totemic and nature spirits, creator heroes, ancestors, gods – or actually embodied the essence of such beings, being simply places of supernatural power.

The spirit of place

The German theologian Rudolf Otto claimed that such sacred places had an eerie quality that he called a 'numen', a divine power, from which the term 'numinosity' was later coined. He felt that this sense of a spirit of place, a genius loci (or as Otto actually called it, a numen loci), was the origin of humanity's association of selected places with holiness.

ABOVE Croagh Patrick, on the west coast of Ireland, has a dramatic, near-perfect pyramidal form, which is especially impressive when viewed from inland with the setting sun behind it. It has been an important pilgrimage site for pagans and Christians since prehistoric times.

Otto wrote that this was acknowledged in Genesis 28 when Jacob sleeps on a stone at Bethel and has his dream-vision of angels on a ladder to heaven and of a powerful entity that he assumes to be God. Afterwards Jacob remarks, 'How fearful is this place! This is none other than the house of Elohim...', and erects as a monolith the stone that he slept on.

The sacred place, Otto argued, is literally an awe-full one.[1] This view is sharply exemplified in the South Pacific island of New Caledonia, where people offer prayers to holy places even before praying to the ancestors.[2]

Anthropologist Lucien Lévy-Bruhl noted that primary peoples venerated 'outstanding and remarkable features of the landscape', which were taken to be indications 'of the presence and the activity (in the past and now) of the mythic ancestors'.[3] In more pragmatic cases, landscape features could be considered holy because they possessed material properties that were useful in ritual and ceremony, such as minerals for paints, or grasses, herbs and trees for incense, healing and dyes.

Generally, the numinous or spirit-dwelling types of sacred places break down into four basic categories: sacred peaks, ritual caves, venerated trees and holy waters, together with a range of other, lesser features, such as specific rock outcrops.

Mountain landmarks

Holy hilltops and mountain summits tended to be distinctive landmarks. For example, Croagh Patrick, on the west coast of Ireland – which was resorted to in pagan, prehistoric times and is still the focus of Christian pilgrimage – has a dramatic, near-perfect pyramidal form visible from great distances, and is profoundly impressive when viewed from inland with a summer sun setting behind it.

Yet another dramatic example of a venerated landmark is England's Glastonbury Tor, a solitary conical hill that rises conspicuously from the flat landscape of the Somerset Levels and which was in fact once an island in a shallow sea. Apart from being a dramatic sight, redolent with a numinosity that still attracts Christian and New Age pilgrims as well as tourists, echoes of the Tor's original sanctity still reverberate through ancient folklore. This states that the singular hill was home to the last King of the Fairies, Gwynn ap Nudd, that it is the entrance to Annwn, the Celtic underworld, and that the spirit of King Arthur leading a rowdy retinue of the undead, the 'Wild Host', rides out at night from Cadbury Castle – a hill 19 km (12 miles) to the east of the Tor, and thought to be the actual location of the

legendary Camelot – scooping up the souls of the dying and depositing them at the foot of the Tor, ready to descend to Annwn. Interestingly, fragments of ancient trackways seem to mark the course that the Wild Host is said to take, and archeologists found an early Bronze Age burial on Cadbury Castle containing the skeleton of a tall male in a ritual boat, its prow pointing to Glastonbury Tor, prominent on the horizon (such boat burials are rare in Britain). Taken together, these fragments of lore surely provide evidence of a mindscape that once focused on the Glastonbury landmark.

ABOVE Glastonbury Tor rises dramatically from the flat landscape of the Somerset Levels in England. Its conspicuous nature led it to be imbued with a numinosity that still attracts people today.

Mountain veneration

Mount Fuji is a national landmark in Japan and is sacred to both Shinto and Buddhist adherents. The Buddhists relate it to the Bodhisattva of Wisdom, while in Shinto tradition it is dedicated to the goddess of flowering trees, Konohana Sakuya Hime. Pilgrims have come to the mountain for at least seven centuries; straw models of the volcano are burned as part of the ceremonies associated with the peak, and a lacquered model of Fuji weighing more than 1 tonne (1 ton) is carried up it slopes during observances (see also pages 58–59).

In the New World a great many mountains were considered sacred. For example, the distinctive 4,369-metre (14,200-foot) Mount Shasta in northern California was venerated by all the Native American groups who lived around its base. It is still held sacred by today's Wintu people, and it is their tradition to orient the body of a person who has just died towards Shasta, so that the soul can fly there and subsequently ascend to the Milky Way. In the country around the mountain there are subtle markers, such as perched boulders on cliff edges, to act as guideposts for the soul on its flight to Shasta.

The sacred mountain of Mexico's Olmec people (c. 1000–600 BCE) was the volcano of San Martin Pajapan, in the Tuxtla Mountains on the Gulf coast of Veracruz. They considered it to be their place of origin. Again, it is a landmark that towers above the surrounding peaks and dominates the area around the sacred lake of Catemaco. In 1897, a life-size statue of a kneeling Olmec ruler was found at the volcano's crater. In La Venta, one of their major centres, the Olmec built a huge effigy of this volcano out of local clay. They fluted the sides of the mound to create a realistic image. This was, in effect, the first of the Meso-American pyramids and was part of a ritual complex that was a constructed analogue of a natural sacred landscape.

Unsurprisingly, mountain veneration was a strong Inca tradition in the Andes of South America. According to the chronicles of the conquering Spanish, people living near a conical peak deformed their heads by binding them as children so as to assume a similar shape. If the sacred mountain happened to be flat-topped, they flattened their heads accordingly. The Inca also sacrificed children on selected high peaks. For instance, on the 6,300-metre (26,000-foot) summit of Mount Ampato in Peru, the deep-frozen body of a young Inca girl of about 14 years of age was found, together with the mummified bodies of two younger children and various artefacts such as bowls and figurines. The girl had been killed by a blow to the head. Again, on Mount Llullaillaco in Argentina, the frozen bodies of a young boy in a red tunic, a teenage girl with braided hair and a younger girl were discovered in a walled area next to stone shelters. They had been allowed to die from exposure, after being plied with coca leaves, and had kept their frozen vigil on the mountains for more than 500 years.

Almost every ancient society around the world had its examples of sacred hills or mountains, and their varying ways of worshipping them.

OPPOSITE **Mount Fuji is sacred to both Shinto and Buddhist adherents. It has been a destination of pilgrimage for centuries and is one of many venerated mountains throughout the world.**

Subterranean mindscapes

Caves were acknowledged as places of sanctity by virtually all peoples everywhere. They were not only places of shelter, but were the first cathedrals, and even today we can feel their numinous power when we descend into them. The cave was traditionally thought of as the gateway to the underworld, the realm of the shades and the shaman – a place of visions, of otherworldly silence, of mind-altering deep darkness.

RIGHT **Detail of a bison and other animals from a Paleolithic mural painting in the caves at Lascaux, France. Underground places where the spirit world was encountered were often marked in such a way.**

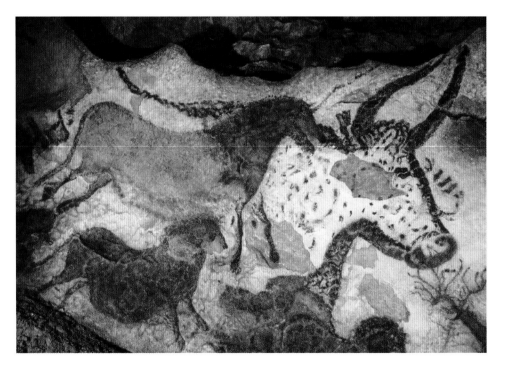

Hints of underworld entities existed in the convoluted forms of stalactites and stalagmites glimpsed in flickering torchlight. This was so from the remotest times, and that is why we have the Old Stone Age, Paleolithic, painted caves of Spain and southern France, such as Lascaux and Chauvet. These places were where the spirit world was encountered, where magic and ritual were born and where the skills of human art emerged.

Charonia and oracles of the dead

A great many caves in Greece and other eastern Mediterranean lands became places for prophetic activities or revelation. Indeed, a cave on the Greek island of Patmos is where St John is said to have had his Revelation in the 1st century CE. The cave is now known as the Holy Grotto of Revelation. Caves were typically seen in ancient Greece as entrances to the underworld, to Hades, and were often referred to as Plutonia or Charonia, after Pluto, lord of the underworld, and Charon, the ferryman of souls across the River Styx.

There were also oracles of the dead, *nekuomanteia*, including a famous one at Avernus near Cumae in southern Italy. In the Meander Valley in Asia Minor there were three celebrated Charonia – at Hierapolis, at Acharaca and at the Aornum near Magnesia. These oracles were located in an area where noxious vapours rose from the ground. The gases could be dangerous and deadly, as well as mind-altering. 'For instance, at Hierapolis (modern Pamukkale) there was a deep cave with a narrow opening filled with misty poisonous vapours, which killed every animal entering the cave,' historian Yulia Ustinova informs us. 'Only the eunuch priests of the goddess Cybele were able to enter the cave, either due to their techniques of holding their breath, or antidotes... The Plutonium has been identified: it is a deep chamber and a hole, emitting highly poisonous gases. Thus, ancient accounts of gas discharge have been verified by modern scientists and found precise.'[4]

Recent investigations at the great oracle centre of Delphi in Greece have similarly identified ground fractures where emissions of mind-altering gases occurred under the temple of Apollo. The ancient Greeks called these *pneuma*, a sacred breath from the earth that inspired the prophetess who held audience there.

Virgin water and ritual activity

Different societies gravitated towards caves for varying reasons. The ancient Maya went deep into the cavern systems of Mexico's Yucatán peninsula to obtain 'virgin water'

for ritual purposes, rather than for drinking. Such water lay in subterranean lagoons that had never seen the light of day or dripped from cave roofs. The Maya also worshipped stalactites and stalagmites, placing special stone troughs beneath them to collect drips of the holy virgin water. To this day some Mayan groups believe that the Earth Lord dwelled in a cave.

The great ruined city of Teotihuacan in the Valley of Mexico, abandoned centuries before even the rise of Mayan civilization, has a giant pyramid, the so-called Pyramid of the Sun, rising out of its midst. This is built over a natural lava-tube cave that had been modified by the artificial lowering of its roof in certain places and the narrowing of parts of its natural passageways (see page 114). It was used for ritual activity before the pyramid was built and was the origin point of the entire city, one of the largest in the world at its time.

ABOVE The Priestess Pythia presided over the Temple of Apollo at Delphi. Her prophecies are thought to have been aided by mind-altering gases emitted from ground fractures under the temple, which the ancient Greeks thought of as sacred breath from the earth.

Root and branch

Because they are more perishable than topographical features, we do not know a great deal about the part that trees played – individually or as copses, groves or forests – in ancient sacred geographies. But we know enough to be sure they were considered important landscape elements in the mindscapes of the past.

ABOVE **Trees were considered imporant landscape elements in the past, an example of which lies at Sea Henge off the east coast of England – a prehistoric timber circle surrounding a great tree.**

Prehistoric sacred trees

We know that the tree was venerated in Minoan Crete, for instance, because of medallions and carvings showing priestesses worshipping individual trees, while in pagan Celtic Ireland a sacred tree was known as a *bile* and the Druids worshipped in sacred groves. Modern archeology in Britain has begun to reveal that Stone Age people built timber temples as well as megalithic sites. Ironically, the megaliths in the world's most famous stone circle, Stonehenge, were handled like timber: mortise and tenon joints secured the great stone lintels onto the giant sarsen uprights, and some of the other stones had even been prepared for tongue-and-groove joints.

More direct evidence for prehistoric sacred trees emerged in 1998 with the discovery of what came to be known as 'Sea Henge', which emerged from tidal sands off the eroding east coast of England. It was a prehistoric timber circle surrounding part of a great tree. When this was pulled out of the sands by lifting equipment, it turned out to be the stump of a giant oak tree that had been placed upside down into the ground with its roots in the air, curiously reminiscent of wooden idols found in Lapland that had been fashioned from inverted tree stumps. Radiocarbon-dating was conducted, linked to the tree's annular rings, to give the accurate finding that it had been felled in the year 2050 BCE.

Boundary rituals

Up until the 19th century the seasonal northward and southward legs of the migratory cycle of the Nenets reindeer herders of Arctic Russia took them through Kozmin Copse twice a year. The slim stand of trees comprising the copse separates areas of tundra, marking a boundary, a ritual threshold zone, between what the Nenets believed to be the female sphere of influence to the north and the male region to the south. In the autumn the women had to undergo various purification rituals

on the journey southwards, while in spring on the return leg of the migration it was the men's turn to do likewise. The trackway through the copse was effectively a pathway shrine, while the trees on either side were venerated and adorned with votive and sacrificial offerings, such as ribbons, small bells, rings and mirrors, many of which are still fixed to the trees.[5]

Vestiges of tree veneration in Europe have survived down into the historical era in a variety of ways. There were special trees at certain locations – Britain's Anglo-Saxon charter of 845 CE mentions 'the ash tree which the ignorant call holy' at Taunton in Somerset. This was possibly a physical symbol of the cosmological Yggdrasil, the mighty ash tree that linked the worlds of the dead, humans and gods in Norse mythology. Some boundary trees were known as 'Gospel Oaks' and became specifically associated with Rogation Day, the Christian festival that marked parish boundaries and blessed the fields and crops – the festival had been adapted from a previous pagan observance. The existing

maypole and German *Maibaum* traditions are faint memories of the sanctity of special trees.

Sacred trees worldwide

The sacred tree figured in the mindscapes of people around the world. In Fiji the tall tavola tree was thought to harbour the war god Ravuravu, and war drums were made from its wood; in Bengal the goddess Durga-Kali is believed to reside in the roots of certain trees, and in the village of Tamdungsa in Nepal's Kathmandu Valley there are two groves, in each of which live, respectively, the divinities Shyhibda and Shyingmardung; to damage the trees in either grove would be to invite disaster. In Madagascar there are said to be three species of tree that can only grow at sacred places, while in India and parts of South-East Asia Buddhists bedeck certain 'bo trees' or fig trees (*Ficus religiosa*) in colourful ribbons, in memory of the tree under which the Buddha sat when he obtained enlightenment.

Although the examples of tree veneration that we know about are many, we will never know the full extent of such worship.

Holy waters and other sacred markers

Of all the key elements in former sacred geographies, water was perhaps the most ubiquitous. Almost everywhere people worshipped lakes and pools, rivers, springs and waterfalls. A vestige of this in the Christian West is the ritual of baptism. Another memory resides in myth, where, in the Arthurian romances, the enigmatic and deeply pagan Lady of the Lake gives and reclaims the magical sword Excalibur.

ABOVE **Water was a key element in former sacred geographies. A vestige of water worship can be seen today in the bathing of Hindus in holy rivers. Here, people bathe and pray in the Ganges.**

Healing centres

The ancient Greeks placed their healing centres and oracle temples at water sources. At Epidaurus, a major Aesculapion (one of hundreds of dream-temples dedicated to the healing god Aesculapius, where people resorted to seek a cure for an ailment or even a serious medical condition), there is a very ancient well beneath the building that housed the special cells where people went to have their healing dreams; and another one at Corinth had nine reservoirs of crystal-clear water, as well as using water imported from a distant hot spring via a special road – the water from that source has been found to be radioactive. At the oracle temple of Dodona, a sacred spring gushed forth from beneath the root of the great oak that stood there, and the murmurings of the emerging water were subject to oracular interpretation.

Sacred springheads

Evidence exists indicating that wells, springs and other holy waters also figured in Britain's later Stone Age, the Neolithic era of prehistory. For instance, the source of most (if not all) of the original stones at Stonehenge, the bluestones, is a rocky, granitic ridge known as Carn Menyn, more than 250 km (150 miles) away in the Preseli Hills of south-west Wales. Around the base of the Carn Menyn outcrops of

Votive offerings, including swords and other weapons, have been recovered from many rivers, even the River Thames. And such apparently minor features as a particular bend in a stream or river could be considered a sacred spot, a *huaca*, by Andean Indians. In Hinduism, the concept of sacred bathing at *tirthas*, fords or crossings, in holy rivers continues.

spotted dolerite, archeologists have recently identified what they call 'enhanced springheads'.[6] Now dry because they are above the present-day spring line, these openings in the southern side of the Carn Menyn ridge were dammed by means of crude rocky walling so that when the water emerged from within the ground, small reservoirs were created, as if the Stone Age people wished to collect the water pure and unsullied from within the earth before it trickled through the rocks and down the hill slopes – perhaps there is an echo here of the Mayan idea of 'virgin water'. Close examination has revealed the remnants of other enhancements of these springheads, such as carved rock art, fallen standing stones and small mounds. A clue to the significance that these springs might have had for the Neolithic people possibly exists in the centuries-old legend claiming that water splashed on the stones of Stonehenge acquires healing properties.

Like the Greeks and the builders of Stonehenge, the later Iron Age Celts similarly regarded springs as holy places, believing them to be entrances to the underworld and haunted by spirits. Pagan Celtic shamans or seers also frequented certain waterfalls, alongside which they would lie down, wrap themselves in animal skins and sleep, seeking prophetic dreams with the white-noise roar of the waters pounding in their ears. Far away in the Amazon Basin, Jivaro Indians still use waterfalls as part of their initiation rituals. Water in all its variegated forms ran through a great many of the sacred geographies of the ancient world.

Other markers in sacred geographies

Apart from these four main types of natural places so often included in ancient spiritual maps, there was a range of other features in the landscape that took on significance for early peoples. Rocky outcrops, seams of quartz, isolated boulders, cliffs – in fact almost any noteworthy feature could become imbued with meaning. The Inca, as a good case in point, identified certain natural rocks and boulders as *huacas*. They served as 'markers of places of ancestral origin, of sites where legendary feats of culture-heroes took place, and of spots where humans and animals were turned into stone', as archeologist Maarten van de Guchte informs us.[7]

Place-names often survive through countless generations, providing echoes of the mythic mapping of ancient landscapes. In Greenland, for instance, Inuit (Eskimo) place-names include Toornaarsutoq, 'the place with lots of spirits', and Angakkussarfik, 'the place of the initiation of the shaman'. In Celtic lands the word 'pap', meaning breast, was often applied to rounded hills and mountains (see page 34), recalling a perception of an Earth Goddess that goes back deep into prehistory. In every land that had an indigenous language, place-names can provide clues to former sacred cartography.

ABOVE An enhanced springhead on Carn Menyn, Preseli, Wales. These openings were dammed, possibly so that the pure water could be collected directly from the spring.

LEFT Waterfalls were considered sacred throughout the ancient world. Jivaro Indians in the Amazon Basin still use waterfalls as part of their initiation rituals.

'Improving on nature'

The casting of a conceptual geography over the physical landscape sufficed for untold centuries, but in some societies human expression became bolder and the natural places became altered, enhanced, modified and, ultimately, mimicked in artificially constructed monuments and temples.

Human interference with venerated natural places began cautiously enough. At first, offerings of votive objects would simply be left at a place, or thrown into the water if it was a sacred river or lake. In 1900, when archeologists first penetrated the Psychro Cave on Mount Dikte in Crete, the legendary birthplace of Zeus, they found bronze and pottery votive objects crammed into every nook and cranny. Then actual, if subtle, changes were made to places: loose shale around weirdly weathered outcrops of rock known as tors on England's Bodmin Moor, for example, was organized into barely noticeable boundaries. And a low wall was laid out near the entrance of the Psychro Cave, marking out a ritual area. Also, some of the stalactites and stalagmites within that deep cave were carved to enhance their likenesses to the gods that people fancied they could see in the convoluted calcite folds. The most common modification of natural places, though, was rock art – rock carvings (petroglyphs) and paintings.

Petroglyphs and paintings

Prehistoric rock art appears on cave walls, cliffs, rocky outcrops, boulders and exposed slabs of table rock. A common motif in outdoor rock art is cup marks – round hollows ground out of the rock surface, often surrounded by enclosing circular grooves and known as 'cup-and-ring marks'. In other variations around the world there is carved and sometimes painted imagery. Cave paintings are well known, but prehistoric paintings on external surfaces are fairly rare. A remarkable survival occurs at Ayers Rock in southern California. This is a boulder as big as a house, to which shamans from all over the Sierra Nevada region resorted for centuries. Multicoloured panels of rock paintings depicting spirit animals and antlered shamans survive on parts of the rock.

Rock art signifies natural places and features as having been considered special in the past, but the meaning of such markings remains elusive. Carved boulders on English moorlands often occur at places that offer wide views, and seem to have been made both by and for hunters. This also seems to have been the case at Chan da Lagoa, Campo Lameiro, in Galicia, Spain. There, certain boulders have carvings depicting reindeer,

BELOW Pre-historic cup and ring marks on a stone at Lordenshaw, Northumberland National Park, England. Although this art indicated the rock or place was special, the exact meaning of such marks remains elusive.

and archeologists have found that these particular rocks happen to mark what are now the routes taken though the landscape by free-ranging wild horses, which, in the past, were probably the ways that deer herds wandered through the country.[8]

Some engraved rocks might also have been signposts for travellers and pilgrims making their way to holy places. Grapevine Canyon at the foot of Dead Mountain in southern Nevada was once the destination for a Yuman tribal pilgrimage, and up until recent centuries tribal shamans would make long journeys to the canyon. The rock art is thought to be a record of the visions experienced by the shamans during their vision quests in the canyon.[9]

Paying respect

When people began to make artificial sacred places they often acknowledged a natural feature that had long held sacred significance for them, as if to pacify it, to let the spirits that dwelled there know that they were still venerated. One way this was done was by imitating the place.

An example is the way the Aztecs in Mexico continued the earlier Olmec tradition of making artificial sacred mountains. The religious complex known as Templo Mayor contained a pyramid with two shrines on its summit, one dedicated to the war god, Huitzilopochtli (see page 47), the other to the rain god, Tlaloc. The pyramid and its shrines were models of Mount Tlaloc and the hill of Tetzcotzingo, both a short distance to the east. These peaks have rock carvings, the remains of temple enclosures and ceremonial ways, rock-cut baths and other features on them showing them to have been converted into ceremonial arenas. In fact, rituals carried out in Templo Mayor were conducted in connection with observances taking place at the same time on Mount Tlaloc.

Another example is the the Akapana, a pyramid built 2,000 years ago by the people of Tiahuanaco, Bolivia. It is surrounded by a moat so as to emulate the sacred Island of the Sun in nearby Lake Titicaca. The pyramid contains materials from distant, venerated, mountain ranges, and has a water system engineered to mimic the way in which water naturally flows down and through mountains, roaring like the thunder among the peaks.[10]

Such respect, indicates that the move away from the ready-made sacred cartography of nature was a tentative one. But the die was cast – humanity had begun to draw new maps of the mind, unfolding new geographies of the soul.

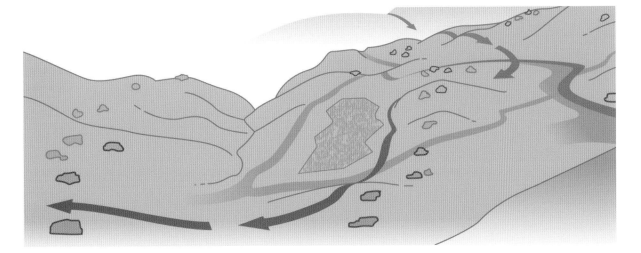

BELOW Chan da Lagoa, Campo Lameiro, in Galicia, Spain. The highlighted rocks display reindeer carvings and the arrows show the route taken through the landscape by wild horses. Based on a drawing by Anxo Rodriguez Paz.

PLACES WITH FACES
Figures in a Landscape

*O*ne of the characteristics that marked a natural place or feature as being sacred to ancient eyes was if its shape presented a likeness to some other form – in a word, if it was simulacrum. A simulacrum is the accidental resemblance to a human face or figure, an animal or a symbolic shape, which is meaningful to the perceiver and seen in the configurations of clouds, the coals of a fire, the bark of a tree or other surface.

The dramatist August Strindberg saw heads as if sculpted out of marble in the creases of bedclothes; Leonardo da Vinci instructed his apprentices to study the 'exquisite landscapes' formed by the mould stains on his studio walls; and the French poet and playwright Antonin Artaud, on the edge of madness, repeatedly saw 'signs, forms and natural effigies' in the plays of light and shadow on crags and rock faces in Mexico. The human mind is geared to try to see patterns in apparent randomness.

Simulacra worldwide

Today we treat such observations as curiosities, as mild, inconsequential diversions, but the willingness to seriously employ such 'double vision' enabled an ancient society to see its mythology emblazoned on its home landscape, to see its deities, cultural heroes or some religious, symbolic icon in the very lie of the land. It mythologized a country, giving it meaning.

The 'Dreamtime' mode of perception

The Australian Aboriginal perception of the topography as being formed by Dreamtime beings is a classic example, and is nowadays probably the best known. Early in the 20th century, for instance, an Anglo-Australian, Olive Pink, was inducted into her local Dreamtime landscape by an Aborigine elder who helped her to recognize topographic *arumba arunga* ('spirit doubles'). Two blue stone rocks, one large, the other smaller, were pointed out to her as 'that mother and baby blue kangaroo'; another was a low hill, the forms of which were said to be the heads of two Dreamtime women who had emerged from and then returned into the ground. 'To the spiritually blind eyes of a non-native, this was simply a low hill, though remarkable because of its isolated white limestone cap on the bronze country... When one's spiritual eyes had been opened ... one could quite well imagine it as the decorated heads of two altjira [Dreamtime] women,' Pink acknowledged.[1]

The scale of simulacra recognized by this 'Dreamtime' mode of perception can range from a small boulder to a rock outcrop or even a whole hillside or mountain range. The Wintu people of northern California consider that 'rock features of unusual configuration' harbour indwelling spirits.[2] In the Andes, a 17th-century Spanish Jesuit, Bernabé Cobo, noted that the Inca 'worshipped the works of nature that were unaltered by human contrivance'. A natural feature, usually a rock, could be seen as a sacred place or *huaca* if it had an 'arresting visual characteristic or peculiar feature' or a resemblance to a human being or a creature such as a falcon.[3] Conversely, *huacas* could sometimes function as 'seats' from which specific mountain peaks could be observed. The Inca even worked body parts into their perceptions of the landscape, so that various shapes of noses could be read into the forms of mountains

and ridges – this was very much tied in with Inca schemes of social hierarchy. Far away in Manitoba, Canada, the Anishinabe people continue to make offerings at Buffalo Rock, a boulder presenting the coincidental likeness of a buffalo at rest. This boulder is located on the fringe of the petroform or boulder-mosaic landscape at Tie Creek, Whiteshell Provincial Park, where small rocks laid down perhaps 15 centuries ago form mysterious patterns across table rock exposed during the last Ice Age (see pages 96–97). While the boulder is a work of nature, it is difficult to doubt that the location for the patterns was selected because of its presence.

Landscape gods in Asia

Parts of the Himalayas were conceived of in sacred geographical terms defined by the occurrence of simulacra. Anthropologist Toni Huber tells us that a Buddhist pilgrim 'who appears to be just staring at a group of boulders may be in the process of a sophisticated landscape interpretation exercise'.[4]

The area of Kaza, the main town of the Spiti Valley, located in the north-eastern

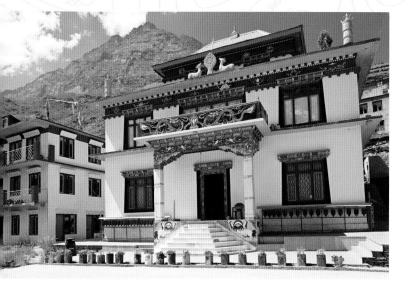

ABOVE Kardang Temple in the Indian Himalayas is a destination of pilgrimage. It was built facing a twin-peaked mountain and a glacier, which together form the appearance of a Buddhist deity.

sector of India's Himalayan hill country of Himachal Pradesh, has a distinctive Buddhist culture. There is 'a "sacred" geography which somehow interpenetrates with the mundane geographical features of the landscape,' states anthropologist Elizabeth Stutchbury. She further explains: 'The yogins [practitioners of yoga] of Karzha, through the tantric practices of Tibetan Buddhism … have transformed ordinary geographical features, such as rivers, caves, rocks and mountains, the macrocosm, into "sacred" places which constitute a … geography conceptualized as a mandala.'[5] An 18th-century poem by a local yogin-saint expresses this:

> *The mountain to the right is like a pile of jewels*
> *The mountain to the left like the fierce deity King of Wrath*
> *The mountain in front like the triangle of origin piled up*
> *The mountain behind like a crouching lion.*

In the same landscape, a twin-peaked mountain and a glacier facing Kardang Temple combine to form the simulacrum of a Buddhist deity that pilgrims come to meditate upon. The face, the eyes and the head of an elephant skin held by the deity are perceivable in the glacier. Another mountain configuration in the region looks like a woman reclining on her back with loose, flowing hair. Indeed, many peaks in the district are perceived as revealing the presence of a sacred being by means of their shapes, as the yogin's poem signifies.

Landscape divination

This way of seeing is linked in this and neighbouring Himalayan regions with observations in which the annual progression of the sun is associated with particular skyline features, and is further extended into a tradition called *satalegpa*, a form of landscape divination that, among other things, places attention on the specific geographical location of buildings. In the relatively nearby Himalayan Golok region of Tibet, for example, the temple of Dodrup Chen is situated within topography that is said to look like a specific Dzogchen master sitting in meditation.

The area of La phyi in south-west Tibet is an important pilgrimage landscape made up of three mountains, one of which is perceived as the body of the deity Vajravarahi, with a rock outcrop known as Ras chen being seen as her head, the Seng khyams rock as her belly, and a rock in front of the bDud'dul cave as her knee. Samvara is another deity seen elsewhere at La phyi in the lie of the land. 'When asked to describe the mountain, local residents and pilgrims indicate rock outcrops which represent the deity's head and shoulders, while ridges on either are said to be his legs, the river that flows south from the place is said to be the stream of his urine, and so forth,' writes Toni Huber, a professor at the University of Berlin.[6]

Temples and simulacra

Other examples of Buddhist sacred landscapes in eastern Asia include one on

Mount Haitang, now a national protected forest park close to Fuxin, Liaoning province, in north-eastern China, and another in Namsan in south-eastern Korea. Each consists of complexes of temples built in mountainous terrain punctuated with Buddhist sculptures.

The core sacred spot on Mount Haitang is a cave that was used by a Tantric Buddhist monk. It is said that early in the Qing Dynasty (1644–1912 CE) a royal surveying party guided by this Mongolian monk, and using various forms of divination including the seeking of rocks of certain shapes, determined the location of what was to be the second-largest temple in the area. This was the Pu'an Temple, now defunct. Around this temple are boulders carved and painted with images of buddhas, bodhisattvas and other deities and holy warriors. They are interspersed with unadorned simulacra, such as Mountain Eagle Rock, Toad Rock, Coiled Dragon Rock and Hat Rock, among many others, their names indicating their accidental resemblances. The complex as a whole, which evolved over two centuries, covers nearly 5 hectares (12 acres) of the mountainside and involves 26 large buildings, 1,500 towers and halls, and 8 km (5 miles) of preaching paths.[7]

Namsan ('Southern Mountain') in Gyeongju province, South Korea, is an oval-shaped massif and now a protected national forest and UNESCO World Heritage Site. Riven by many valleys, it was co-opted by Buddhism in the 6th century CE, although it was sacred before then – shamans conducted rain dances there, and megalithic monuments dating to the 1st millennium BCE have been found. There is evidence that certain places on Namsan were used for making offerings to nature spirits, so it is perhaps not surprising that the Buddhists believed that Namsan harboured many buddhas and bodhisattvas that had descended from heaven to dwell

in its rocks and trees. A probable reason that the mountain was such a spiritual focus was the presence of many granite rocks scattered over it and resembling animals and objects.[8] They are known by such names as Old Man, Python, Fierce Tiger, Lion, Big Bear, Boar, Cat and even Dung Rock, and occur primarily in the Yongjang Valley. Namsan is home to more than a hundred temples, most of them now archeological sites, 63 pagodas, nearly 40 statues and about 90 sculpted rocks, the largest of which is the 10-metre (30-foot) Buddha Rock in the T'ap Valley.

ABOVE **In line with a Himalayan tradition called** *satalegpa*, **the temple of Dodrup Chen in Tibet is situated within topography thought by adherents to be reminiscent of a Dzogchen master in meditation.**

BOROBUDUR

The recognition of simulacra was widespread in Asia, so even on Java, Indonesia, it is noted with regard to the great temple of Borobudur. This huge Buddhist temple, built *c.* 800 CE and situated on Java's central Kedu Plain, consists of platforms and terraces surmounted by a giant stupa or dome-shaped building. More than 500 statues of the Buddha adorn the complex. Long-established local tradition states that a particular section of the Menoreh mountain range, visible on the southern horizon from the temple, depicts the original architect of Borobudur, Gunadharma. When viewed from the top of the temple, the ridgeline does indeed resemble the form of a man lying on his back, with his facial profile clearly discernible.[9]

Iconic simulacra

The prominent rounded hill of Tidar on the Kedu Plain in Java, close to the city of Magelang, is a landmark known as the 'Nail of Java' on account of its appearance, and in legend it fixes the island of Java to its present location, for it is said that long ago Java was simply floating on the ocean and could not be lived on until it was nailed firmly to the seabed. This is an example of a landscape feature that resembles not a human or animal form, but a cultural symbol of some kind.

ABOVE The giant calcite simulacrum of a tree inside the Mayan ritual cave of Balankanché. Surrounded by ancient censers, the blackened area of the "tree trunk" was caused by smoke from the burning of copal incense.

RIGHT The shape of cleft-peaked mountains is visible in Minoan artefacts, such as the Horns of Consecration at the Palace of Knossos.

Another, quite startling example, this time in the Americas, is to be found inside the Mayan ritual cave of Balankanché, in the Yucatán, Mexico, near the ancient Mayan ceremonial city of Chichén Itzá. The main natural passageway leads into a great circular cavern with a curiously domed floor rising in the centre. There, linking the cavern's ceiling and the dome's crest, is a giant fused stalactite and stalagmite looking remarkably like a tree trunk, with the impression of foliage created by countless small, spiky stalactites. This calcite 'tree' is surrounded by stone and wooden figures, pottery incense burners, small pots and other votive objects. Carbon-dating of charcoal from a censer and a hearth suggested a 9th-century date for the placing of the objects. This striking tree-like formation was therefore clearly worshipped by the ancient Maya, who doubtless would have seen it as a representation of the Mayan 'World Tree' concept, Wakah-Chan ('Raised-up-Sky'), provided by the earth itself. Sacred geography could exist underground as well as above.

Cleft- and saddle-peak mountains
The suggestive forms of configurations in the landscape were undoubtedly recognized by ancient peoples, but in some cases they might even have suggested an icon to a society. It is hard to determine such chicken-and-egg situations in some civilizations, such as those on Crete and in Egypt.

The Bronze Age Minoans of Crete had an iconic relationship with cleft-peak mountains. Their palace temples align with or stand in sight of such distinctive peaks, and they built shrines on their summits (see page 14). Phaistos, as one example, aligns to the saddle-shaped summit of Mount Ida, in which there are caves that

ABOVE The temples of Bronze Age Minoans were built to align with or be in sight of cleft- or saddle-peaked mountains. There is some evidence to suggest that this shape represented a landscape goddess. This is the view of Mount Psiloritis (Ida) from Phaistos. The dark round shape a little way below the right peak is the entrance to the sacred cave of Kamares.

were used even prior to the time of the palaces for goddess worship. The main cave there, Kamares, was where the legendary Cretan shaman-figure, Epimenides, went into a trance and became master of 'enthusiastic wisdom' – in other words, expert in the techniques of inducing altered states of consciousness. The palace of Mallia is directed at Mount Dikte, which also has a split peak, and Knossos is overlooked by the cleft peak of Mount Juktas, which the great archeologist of Minoan Crete, Sir Arthur Evans, noted looked like a man's head gazing skywards, when viewed from the direction of Tylissos – he learned that the locals there called it the 'Head of Zeus'.

But the repeated cleft- or saddle-peak configuration seems to have held a deeper significance for the Minoans. The American art historian Vincent Scully put forward the idea that this shape was originally seen as representing a landscape goddess. 'These features create a profile which is basically that of a pair of horns, but it may sometimes also suggest raised arms or wings, the female cleft, or even, at some sites, a pair of breasts,'

he wrote.[10] There is some evidence for this, such as a depiction on an artefact found at Knossos of a woman standing on a mountain with sacral horns in the background. Did such topographic forms prompt the sacred iconography of the Minoans, visible in such artefacts as their 'Horns of Consecration', the ritual double-axe or labrys, which is ubiquitous in Minoan temple imagery, as well as the upraised-arms salute depicted time and again in Minoan figurines?

The visual association of temple locations with twin-peaked mountains eventually found its way onto mainland Greece. A classic example is the Mystery temple of Eleusis, standing at a spot west of Athens where in legend Persephone (Kore) was abducted into the underworld and where her mother, Demeter, mourned for her. The strongly cleft peak of Mount Kerata ('Horns') dominates the horizon and is clearly visible from the temple precincts. Or, again, the sacred twin peaks of Mount Hymettos are noticeably visible on the eastern skyline from the summit of the Acropolis at Athens.

Pyramids

The same open question as to whether shapes in the landscape informed religious imagery or whether such imagery was projected onto landscape features occurs with regard to that powerful icon of ancient Egypt, the pyramid.

On the western side of the River Nile opposite present-day Luxor is the great royal necropolis known as the Valley of the Kings. This exists within the folds of a massif dominated by a peak known as el-Qurn, 'the Horn'. This is of a near-perfect pyramidal form, and it has been suggested that it was this that inspired the architects of ancient Egypt to create their monumental pyramids. And the possible role of simulacra goes further at this place. One bay in the massif, Deir el-Bahri, was sacred to Hathor, the goddess who was Mistress of the West and was often shown as a cow, or as a woman with cow's ears and horns. It was believed that she materialized out of the mountain to receive the souls of the dead kings. She was also sometimes depicted as a cobra, the symbol of royal power in ancient Egypt. (This was probably a throwback to an earlier, pre-dynastic deity called Meresger, 'She Who Loves Silence', a cobra goddess who was believed to dwell within the mountain.) In the shrine of Hathor within the temple of Thuthmosis III in Deir el-Bahri, a statue was found showing the pharaoh Amenophis II being brought forth by the goddess in her cow form and suckled by her, while across the Nile in the great temple complex of Karnak, adjacent to Luxor, Amenophis II is shown with a cobra wearing horns.

Also within the terminal bay of Deir el-Bahri is the vast New Kingdom temple of Queen Hatshepsut. This happens to be positioned at the foot of a rock column that

obtrudes from a cliff. No one saw anything
special about this cliff-face until 1991, when
Egyptologist V. A. Donohue perceived that
the forms within the rock column 'simulate
the configuration of a statue-group in which
the cobra, its eyes and the lateral markings
on the underside of its distended hood clearly
observable, rears to the full height of the cliffs
behind a standing anthropomorphic figure,
either sovereign or deity, who wears the
head-dress and beard'.[11] This configuration is
badly eroded but still discernible, especially
when the angle of the sun enables light and
shadow to enhance it. It should be noted that
Hatshepsut was known for her landscaping
skills, and that the main axis of Karnak aligns
across the Nile towards her temple.

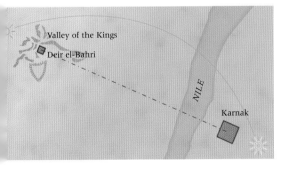

LEFT Queen Hatshepsut was
known for her landscaping
skills, and it is seen as no
cooincidence that the main
axis of Karnak aligns across
the Nile towards her temple.

ABOVE The New Kingdom
temple of Queen Hatshepsut
lies at the foot of a rock
column, within which the
forms of a hooded cobra and
a deity with head-dress and
beard are discernable.

Stone Age simulacra

A vivid simulacrum in Scotland allows us a glimpse into the Neolithic mind. The Kintyre peninsula on the west coast hosts a group of three standing stones known as Ballochroy. The central stone has its broadest side aligning towards two rounded peaks on the island of Jura, almost 32 km (20 miles) offshore. These are known as the Paps of Jura, and the sun sets behind them at the summer solstice when viewed from Ballochroy.

As we have already seen, 'pap' is an archaic word for breast, and the likeness of the two Jura mountains to a pair of breasts must have been noted for thousands of years and they were probably seen as a manifestation of some version of an Earth Mother goddess.

Other Paps alignments
This interpretation is reinforced by another Stone Age sightline to the Paps. On the island of Islay, which almost touches the southern shore of Jura, there is a lake, Loch Finlaggan, with the remains of Stone Age monuments around its shores. Especially significant is a standing stone, which archeological investigation has revealed once had a row of stones leading up to it. Looking along the alignment of this row to the surviving large standing stone, the eye is led directly to the domed summits of the Paps on the closely adjacent Jura. From Finlaggan they project dramatically and in isolation above an intervening ridge to the north-east.

Similar rounded peaks are located near Killarney on the west coast of Ireland. Known as the Paps of Anu, they rise prominently due to their relative isolation and their symmetry and roundness. In myth, Anu was the mother of the last generation of gods who ruled the earth, the Tuatha De Danaan. Celtic scholar Anne Ross writes that the hills manifest the presence of the goddess embedded in the land, and remarks that Anu is still regarded as the local fairy queen. People still gather here at Lughnasa, the pagan Celtic festival held in early August (superseded by the Christian harvest-time observance of Lammas), and climb the hills.[12]

Rocks as human forms
Another kind of simulacrum exists in the completely different context of the Externsteine rocks, a group of five tall,

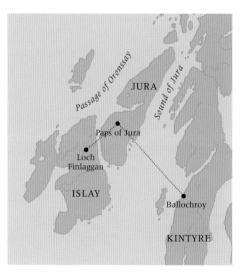

RIGHT The significance of the Paps of Jura is confirmed by two separate alignments of Stone Age monuments on the mainland and an adjacent island.

weathered fingers of sandstone located in the Teutoberger Wald district near Detmold, Germany. Near the top of the tallest pillar (Tower Rock) is a rock-hewn chapel, either pagan or early Christian, with a round window through which the midsummer rising sun shines. Near the base of another pillar there is a relief panel carved in the medieval period showing Christ's descent from the cross, confirming the Christianization of the site. During the 20th century the Externsteine became a centre for the Nazi SS, revealed by the engraved image of the German eagle in a rock face. There is some evidence of the presence of reindeer hunters at the rocks far back in prehistory, but the early history of the site is uncertain. There are some claims that the place was a focus for pagan worship until Christianization by Charlemagne in 772 CE.

What is certain, though, is that on the side of one of the rock columns there is an overhanging segment that from most angles looks like a human figure with its arms raised, as if tied to the rock.

This natural feature has long been the source of speculation, including suggestions that it was seen as being a naturally occurring depiction of the pagan north-European god Odin, hanging on the Norse version of the primordial World Tree, Yggdrasil, which in myth he did for nine nights in order to gain the secret of the runes. Some commentators have argued that the feature was 'Christianized' by the addition of an artificial hole, representing the spear wound made in Christ's side as he hung on the cross. If this is correct, then it may be the only known case of the Christianization of a simulacrum.

ABOVE The Paps of Jura, Scotland. For Stone Age Europeans these mountains were a manifestation of the Earth Mother Goddess.

Another example of a rock resemblance to a human form occurs in England, on the Cornish hill of Carn Brea. On the summit are the vestiges of an early Neolithic settlement near a great granite outcrop that presents the natural, unworked appearance of a head, complete with brow, cheekbones and lips. Known as the Carn Brea Giant, this natural rocky visage faces out towards another hill, St Agnes's Beacon, 10 km (6 miles) away. In a legend reminiscent of some Aboriginal Dreamtime myth, it is said that there was also a giant on the beacon, whose name was Bolster. The giants threw rocks at one another until Bolster ran out of ammunition, thus explaining why St Agnes's Beacon is devoid of rocks and Carn Brea is littered with them.

Other anthropomorphic forms

In Stone Age Europe, as elsewhere, simulacra could be on a small scale as well as large, as is testified by the tradition of Saami seite stones, natural rocks sometimes forming *siejddes* (sacrificial sites), in Lapland. These rocks often became identified as

sacred because they bore a resemblance to humans, animals or birds.[13] Some of them could also be seen as suggesting the forms of otherworldly beings.

Roughly similar features occurred in a lonely, uninhabited corner of remote Glen Lyon in Scotland, where scholars believe that a pagan Celtic observance has been maintained at a kind of shrine in an unbroken line from at least late prehistory until very recent years. The 'shrine' is a tiny stone structure known as Tigh nam Bodach, 'The Hag's House'. In early May (Beltane in the Celtic calendar) a lone shepherd taking his animals up to pasture would take a group of curiously shaped stones out of the house and stand them up in front of it. Every early November (the Celtic Samhain) they were put back inside for the winter. The stones are mainly water-eroded into archaic likenesses of human forms. They were seen as representing a goddess – the Cailliche, or Old Woman – and her husband and daughter. Three other stones have been added in relatively recent times because 'her family has grown'. In legend, the goddess, who was pregnant, entered the glen along with her husband during a terrible snowstorm. The people of the glen made them a shelter. She had the baby and then stayed in the glen, blessing the people for their kindness. Although some of the stones show signs of having been artificially enhanced, the Cailliche stone itself, about 46 cm (18 inches) tall, is naturally anthropomorphic, though there are faint traces of a face having been inscribed on her 'head', and possibly of a torc round her neck.[14] The rocks came from a nearby stream known as the Cailliche Burn, which is part of a whole mythologized landscape in this part of the glen.[15]

Suggestive forms at Avebury

Finally, in Wiltshire, southern England, there may exist a Stone Age landscape

containing simulacra that have not yet been fully acknowledged by archeologists. It comprises the megalithic monuments forming an extensive Neolithic landscape at Avebury, about 32 km (20 miles) north of the more famous Stonehenge.

The main Avebury monument is a large henge, a roughly circular ditch-and-bank enclosure, containing the world's largest stone circle, with the remnants of various stone settings within its circumference. In the surrounding landscape there are other monuments, including the surviving stones of two approximately parallel rows, the Kennet Avenue, running from the henge's southern entrance. Visitors sometimes note in passing that certain stones in the circle and avenue suggest human or animal forms. Alexander Keiller, who restored some of the Avebury complex in the 1930s, was more specific about this, as he indicated in a 1936 issue of *Antiquity*: 'There can be no question that the stones were dressed to conform to certain required shapes, and to this end were selected as near to the required form as possible.' He was mainly referring to certain opposed stones in the Kennet Avenue, where pillar-shaped stones on one side of the avenue face a lozenge- or diamond-shaped megalith on the other, and speculated that these might symbolize male and female respectively.[16] However, there are other standing stones in the Avebury complex, probably entirely unworked, that look like animals such as a lion and various human faces and forms, especially one in the Kennet Avenue that is so distinctive it cannot but have been perceived as special by those who selected and erected it. Sometimes referred to as the 'Hag stone', it is strongly reminiscent of a Saami seite stone (see page 36).

If we can readily see suggestive forms in some of the Avebury megaliths, so

presumably could the Neolithic builders of the monument. Whether or not certain stones have been dressed, some of them may have been selected because of their basic shapes (as distinct from subsequent weathering effects). It is unquestionably important to guard against wanton flights of fancy, but if we look carefully – as if through ancient eyes – we can perhaps still catch authentic glimpses of the old gods of the Stone Age.

ABOVE One of the three faces people claim to see in the curious stone in the West Kennet Avenue, at Avebury near Stonehenge in the UK.

CENTRE PLACE
Mind, Body, Land

An extremely widespread concept in sacred geography was that of a world centre – a 'world navel' or omphalos; *or, in its vertical extension, a world axis, an* axis mundi. *It was woven into myth, ritual and cosmologies, being envisaged by various peoples in many symbolic forms, including a cosmic mountain, a primordial tree, a giant arrow stuck into the earth, a cosmological bread basket, a stone or rock, the pole star, the hearth or smoke hole in a yurt or other dwelling, and even a pit in the ground.*

The world centre was a way of metaphorically and psychologically locating oneself and one's people in the world, and was conceived as operating at varying levels in different societies – landscape, town, temple and even dwelling. Some cultures had a number of world centres in their territory. Because we have lost the world-centre notion in our modern culture, it can seem to us to be a bizarre and inconsequential fixation, yet it was one of the deepest and most powerful ideas right across the ancient world.

Conceptual centres

*Today, operating on the basis of place as **topos** rather than as **chora** (see pages 8–9), we tend to think of a centre location in strictly measurable, geographical terms – a literal centre. This is not a prerequisite for the notion of the 'world navel', which was conceptual rather than literal. Nevertheless, some physical 'navels' did approximate spatially to central locations, as was the case with the now-vanished, mysterious Etruscans of northern Italy.*

The Etruscans and Romans

When founding a town, the Etruscans dug a pit or shaft and laid out the street grid from it. The pit was supposed in myth to reach down to the underworld and was capped by a large stone, which was lifted only on special days when the dead were allowed to wander among the living, or when the first fruits were cast into the shaft as a harvest offering.

The Romans adopted many traditions of the Etruscans, and in legend it is said that Etruscan surveyors or geomancers laid out the foundations of Rome. The central pit was called *mundus* by the Romans, meaning world or universe, and possibly echoing whatever the Etruscan word for the shaft had been. The Romans always put a *mundus* at the centre of their towns, and even of their military camps. It marked the crossing point of the foundational north–south (*cardo*) and east–west (*decumanus*) roads. *Cardo* gives us the root of the word 'cardinal' – as in the cardinal points of the compass, north and south, east and west. In Roman-founded British market towns, the *mundus* location came to be called the 'Cross' or 'High Cross'.

Ireland

World-centre locations that more loosely approximate to literal centres would include the scheme that operated in the pagan Celtic landscape of Ireland, which was divided into four ancient provinces (Ulster, Munster, Leinster and Connacht) that met in the centre, Mide, where stands the hill of Uisneach – now in the modern County Westmeath). A large natural boulder called Aill na Mireann, the 'Stone of Divisions', is to be found on the hill's slopes. It is not exactly geographically central, but close enough to carry the symbolism.

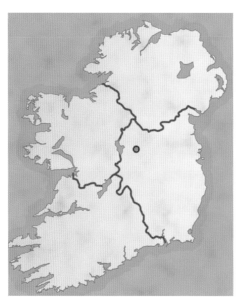

RIGHT The omphalos of Ireland, Aill na Mireann, the 'Stone of Divisions', is found almost at the geographic centre of Ireland, where the four ancient provinces met.

Jerusalem

Again, it could be argued that Jerusalem serves a similar joint role, for while the general region around the eastern end of the Mediterranean has been claimed to be roughly central to the world's landmasses, the city is also of central significance to the Abrahamic religions of Judaism, Christianity and Islam. For Judaism, Temple Mount is the *omphalos* in Jerusalem, being the site of a succession of temples from prehistoric times, including the legendary Temple of Solomon, built to house the Ark of the Covenant. Paul Isaac Hershon's *A Talmudic Miscellany* has a passage that puts it plainly:

The land of Israel is situated in the centre of the world, and Jerusalem in the centre of the land of Israel, and the Temple in the centre of Jerusalem, and the Holy of Holies in the centre of the Temple, and the foundation stone on which the world was founded is situated in front of the ark.

For Christianity, the world navel is the hill of Golgotha in Jerusalem, with the Church of the Holy Sepulchre there containing a stone that used to be referred to as 'the Compass of the Lord', revealing its world-centre association.

The Islamic tradition is that Mohammed, astride the winged steed that took him on his Night Journey from Mecca, alighted on the slab of rock atop Temple Mount (now covered by the Dome of the Rock mosque) and ascended to heaven from there by means of a ladder of light. Two depressions in the rock are said to be the footprints left by the Prophet as he started his ascent. So the site is of great importance to Islam, but the key world navel for this religion is, of course, Mecca, which has eight paths radiating out from the holy sanctuary of the Ka'ba in the precinct of the al-Harram Mosque to the four cardinal and four intermediate directions, thus expressing world-centre symbolism.

BELOW Jerusalem can be seen as the centre of the world for the Abrahamic religions. Temple Mount, now covered by The Dome of the Rock, pictured, is of particular significance to Judaism and Islam.

Symbolic centres

While some ancient world centres were close to being in geographically central positions, the core concept was a deeper one; it really operated at the level of symbolic space. This can be seen in the classic example of the **omphaloi***, navel stones, of ancient Greece. These were generally dome-shaped stones placed at numerous Greek temples, marking such places as symbolic world or cosmological centres.*

ABOVE The omphalos stone in the museum at Delphi, Greece. Navel stones in Ancient Greece marked symbolic world or cosmological centres.

RIGHT Mount Kailas is the physical representation of the Hindu mythic mound, Mount Meru. Indian towns were all planned with a symbolic representation of Mount Meru in the form of a temple in their centres.

Delphi

The oracle temple of Delphi has two surviving navel stones. One, said to be a Roman copy of the original and now located in the site museum, is a sandy-coloured rock about 1 metre (3 feet) tall carved with a mysterious interlacing pattern known as an *agrenon* or net, while the other is a quartz-veined, smooth grey stone looking incongruously like a rocket's nose-cone, now placed alongside the Sacred Way that weaves up through the sloping precinct of the temple complex.

Coins from Delphi show a python coiled round an *omphalos* stone, a symbol of the Earth Goddess, or sat upon by the usurper of that tradition, Apollo. A carved stone tablet from Sparta depicts an *omphalos* stone with a bird on either side of it, each facing in an opposite direction to the other: this refers to a legend about two birds (variously recorded as eagles, ravens or swans) belonging to the god Zeus, who released them from opposite ends of the earth in order to determine the centre of the world by observing where the birds' flight paths crossed.

Mount Meru

Oriental cultures often adopted the image of a mythical mountain as their world navel. Indian (Hindu) cosmology has the

mythic Mount Meru – represented physically by the Himalayan peak of Mount Kailas (venerated by Buddhists as Mount Sumeru), which is the source of the sacred Indus and Brahmaputra rivers. Indian towns were planned out in the image of the idealized universe, with a symbolic representation of Mount Meru in the form of a temple in their centres – all Hindu temples are symbolic representations of Mount Meru. Java's huge Borobudur temple (see also page 29) was designed to symbolize the mythical mountain, and happens to be situated close to the geographical centre of the island, while the walls and moats of the city of Angkor in Cambodia represent the world surrounded by its chain of mountains and the cosmic ocean, and the temple in the centre represents Mount Meru.

The World Tree

In northern Europe and Asia, the world centre was typically pictured as a world axis of some kind, usually a World Tree. The Yakuts of north-eastern Siberia, for example, believed there was a tree with eight branches standing at the 'golden navel of the earth'. For such nomadic reindeer-herder tribes, the tent pole was often regarded as the physical representation of the World Tree – the Soyot and Buryat peoples referred to the tent pole as the Sky Pillar and considered it sacred, placing offerings on small stone altars at the bases of their tent poles. The veneration of the central post is, or was, to be found in many other peoples' dwellings too: those of the Ainu of the northern Japanese islands of Hokkaido and Sakhalin, of many Native American peoples and of the Khasi of north-eastern India.

As has already been noted (see page 19), the Scandinavian and northern European World Tree is Yggdrasil, the primordial ash whose branches reach up to the heavenworld (Asgard) and whose three-branched roots reach down into the underworld, variously to the Well of Fate (Urdr or Wyrd), the spring of Wisdom (Mimir) and the goddess Hel's realm of the dead (Niflheim), from where the Hvergelmir spring gushes forth, feeding the waters of earth and creating the flow of time. The human world (Midgard) is located on the trunk of the tree midway between the branches and the roots.

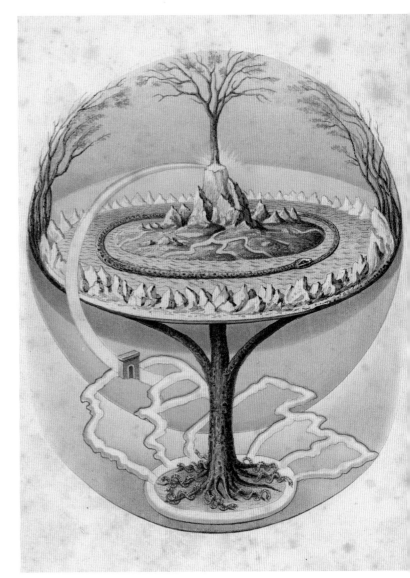

ABOVE The World Tree is a familar concept throughout northern Europe and Asia. The Scandinavian World Tree is Yggdrasil, which represents the relation between the heavenworld, the human world and the underworld.

Middle Place

The notion of the centre and the Four Directions was an ingrained mental template almost everywhere in ancient, pre-Columbian America. Although many Native American Four Directions relate to the compass or cardinal points, some originally related to the sun's positions at key points through the year – eastwards, the most northerly sunrise at the summer solstice and the most southerly sunrise at the winter solstice, and westwards, the sun's corresponding setting points.

In this scheme, the compass points provided four more intervening directions and so, if envisaged as a diagram, the solar directions form the corners of a square and the cardinal directions form a cross within the square.

The basic Native American Four Directions scheme was actually usually conceived of as Six Directions – the Four Directions plus up (above; the sky; the sun at noon) and down (below; the Earth; the sun beneath the feet at midnight). This up–down addition provided a vertical axis, effectively the *axis mundi*.

The 'point of emergence'

In many (if not most) Native American nations all this is related to the belief in a 'point of emergence'. This is a location where a nation's First People emerged from within the ground or from out of a body of water in mythic time, coming from an earlier 'World', 'Sun' or 'Earth' into this one. This point of emergence gives a deeper significance to the concept of 'down', and is symbolized by a small hole called the *sipapu* in the floors of the subterranean ritual and ceremonial chambers known as *kivas* belonging to the Pueblo people of the south-western United States. After emerging, the First People encounter and are helped by creator beings during a migration to their present home. This is illustrated by the Zuni emergence myth (see boxed text opposite).

The sacred geography of the Keres

The Keres people are neighbours of the Tewa, and live in a scattering of *pueblo* villages on the Rio Grande and the Rio Jemez between present-day Albuquerque and Santa Fe in New Mexico. They form a

BELOW The Keres people of modern-day New Mexico represent their complex sacred geography with shrines and natural features in the topography around their villages. (After James Snead and Robert Preucel.)

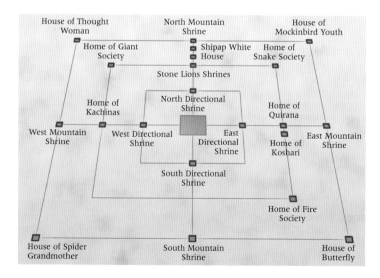

distinct linguistic and cultural group, and their *pueblos* all share a common migration myth, which says that the Keres emerged from an opening in the ground called *shipap* to the north of their present territory.

They have developed a detailed sacred geography using natural features mixed with constructed shrines.[2] Powerful supernatural beings are envisaged as being at the corners of the cosmogram (a flat geometric figure depicting a cosmology) that the Keres have invested in the topography surrounding their villages – male deities on the east, female on the west. In the cardinal directions there are four sacred mountains, on each of which live deities responsible for the weather and the seasons. Each mountain is also associated with its own colour, animal and tree. Although the mountains are of shared sanctity among the Keres, the symbolism of their position can vary, depending on the geographical location of a *pueblo*. So one of the mountains, Mount Taylor, for instance, can be the sacred mountain of the west to one *pueblo*, yet to another it is the holy peak of the north. The venerated mountains are further sanctified by having shrines on their summits; the one on Mount Taylor takes the form of a shallow pit more than 1 metre (3 feet) across.

Between the venerated mountains on the perceived rim of the sacred landscape and each village are the 'houses' of certain supernatural beings, often located in caves or at springs. Pilgrimages are made to them. The detail of the Keres' sacred landscape continues down to the scale of the villages themselves. On the outskirts of each one there are shrines placed in the four cardinal directions. These are usually keyhole-shaped structures with north-facing openings, and villagers can make offerings at them. Finally, there are sets of shrines within the villages' boundaries, the most important ones being in the main plazas. These shrines are seen as being protective against evil influences.

THE ZUNI EMERGENCE MYTH

According to this myth, the first Zuni people emerged from a place deep within the Grand Canyon near Ribbon Falls. They encountered K'yan asdebi, Water Skate, who showed them the Four Directions by spreading out his long legs. His heart and navel indicated 'the midmost place of the Earth-mother'. The First People then left the canyon and wandered off in search of the Idiwana'a, 'Middle Place', to found a permanent home. On their journey they built villages and shrines, made offerings and buried their dead. At the junction of the Little Colorado and Zuni rivers, the wanderers 'had important interactions' with spiritual beings, and the spot became the place that all Zunis go to after death – 'Zuni Heaven'.[1] Eventually, Middle Place was located near the source of the Zuni River and the people settled there. This is the present location of Zuni Pueblo (south of Gallup in New Mexico). Similarly, the Tewa of the Eastern Pueblos of New Mexico consider their village to be 'Earth Mother, Earth Navel, Middle Place'.

Cahokia's ceremonial landscape

That the Four Directions and centre cosmogram was operative from pre-Columbian times (American prehistory) is evidenced by ruins left in the archeological record of the Americas. An example is found at the site of the city and ritual complex of Cahokia, in present-day southern Illinois, the capital of the Mississippian culture between *c.* 1000 and 1400 CE.

Its central feature is the slumped, but still impressive Monks Mound, more than 30 metres (100 feet) in height. It was the hub of the sacred geography of Cahokia's ceremonial landscape, the centre point of the Four Directions. This is emphasized by eight enigmatic ridge-topped mounds in the complex. Their primary role seems to have been to act as symbolic geographical markers, for five of them define the extreme limits of the ceremonial area around Monks Mound, and three of them align with the great mound to form a meridian – Cahokia was laid out to the cardinal points. The remains of a temple were uncovered on the south-west corner of the first terrace of Monks Mound, a position that is precisely on the course of

the meridian. Running south from this position on Monks Mound, the meridian passes through a ridge-top mound, on through another ridge mound and terminates in the south at a massive ridge mound known as Rattlesnake Mound.

On the summit of Monks Mound there had once stood a large timber building, thought to have been the chieftain's house, next to which stood a mighty timber post that would have formed a highly visible landmark. The Cahokian chieftain or king may well have been considered divine or semi-divine, a 'son of the sun', as is known to have been the case in other Native American tribes such as the Natchez of Louisiana, where the chief, the Great Sun, would emerge from his dwelling (also located on a mound), howl three times and then blow tobacco smoke towards the rising sun, then breathe out smoke in the other three directions. At Cahokia such symbolism would have been reinforced by what had been a circle of tall timber uprights surrounding an off-centre post to the west of Monks Mound. Reconstructing the circle using the original postholes – all that remained of the original timber ring – archeologists figured out that a sun-watcher priest standing at the inner post and looking east would have seen the equinoctial sun (21 March and 21 September) rise over the bulk of Monks Mound.

Tenochtitlán

The sense of sacred directionality was etched into the native mind throughout the Americas. A long way south of Cahokia was the capital of the Aztecs, Tenochtitlán, the remains of which now lie beneath modern Mexico City. By the 15th century it had become an independent state with a population of more than 200,000, and ruled over the whole valley.

This great island city containing palaces, plazas and pyramids was laid out to the compass points. The higher ground at

ABOVE The Monk's Mound was the centre point of the Four Directions and, therefore, the hub of the sacred geography of the city of Cahokia in pre-Columbian times.

the centre of Tenochtitlán was the administrative and spiritual heart of the Aztec empire, and the centre of the Aztecs' conceptual universe. Dominating this centre was the Great Temple (Templo Mayor), a twin-shrined pyramid dedicated to the solar war god, Huitzilopochtli, and the storm god, Tlaloc (see page 23). This huge temple stood on the divined spot, the very foundation point, of the city, and had been built over seven times, as archeologists discovered when they excavated its remains – the full extent of which were found by accident beneath a corner of the *zocalo*, or main plaza, of Mexico City, alongside the cathedral. The modern city still bears the stamp of the quadripartite scheme of Tenochtitlán.

Mayan and Incan world centres

Further south still, and further back in time, the ancient Maya likewise had a world-centre cosmology. Apart from a World Tree concept, they also marked the sacred centre in their ceremonial cities. As Mayan scholar David Freidel discovered, this was often a subtle centre. So in the Mayan city of Cerros in Belize, as a case in point, he found that it was marked by a small pyramid that had degenerated into a nondescript mound, dwarfed by the surrounding Mayan

ceremonial architecture. But excavation revealed it to have been a royal temple, dating to the foundation of Cerros. This 'small, unimpressive bump', as Freidel described it, 'turned out to be the pivotal building that anchored everything else'.[3] He found such subtlety repeatedly in the Mayan world, and it still survives. The people of the municipality of San Lorenzo Zincantán, Chiapas, Mexico, told him that they consider a small hill nestling among larger mountains around to be *mixik' balamil*, the navel of the world.

In Mayan cosmology, certain gods support the corners of the universe and designate its centre. This pattern is reprised even today in houses that have corner posts representing the Four Directions, and in fields that have cross-shrines at their corners and centres. All are points of ritual importance.

In South America the world-centre scheme was equally strong. An illustrative pointer to this is Cuzco, the Andean capital of the Inca empire, Tahuantinsuyu, Land of the Four Quarters. The city mirrored the empire's quadripartite plan, being itself divided into four quarters or *suyus*, but in this culture the Four Directions were intercardinal rather than the four compass points (for the reason, see page 44).

The body and beyond

To the Oglala Sioux, Mount Harney in South Dakota was the centre of the world. This location became famous because of the 'Great Vision' seen by the Oglala Sioux holy man, Black Elk, when he was taken up in spirit (or in a near-death experience, as we might say today) to the top of the mountain when seriously ill as a child.

ABOVE Harney Peak, Custer State Park, South Dakota: the world centre for the Oglala Sioux. The famous 'Great Vision' of the holy man Black Elk put the peak at his world centre.

His vision is replete with powerful and haunting symbolism of the centre and the Six Directions: he met the 'Grandfathers' or powers 'of the Four Directions and of the sky and of the Earth'. Although Harney Peak was the physical representative of the world axis for his experience, the wise old shaman remarked that 'anywhere is the centre of the world'.[4] And that is the secret.

The search for the centre

The world-centre concept was so universal because it was essentially the projection of human physiology and neuropsychology outwards onto the land. The upright human being is an axis with four bodily directions (front, back, left, right) extended outwardly in the world-centre scheme and translated into the cardinal directions. The world centre is 'here', which is portable – wherever you are, you are always here. It is paradoxically both a specific and yet non-existent locus.

This is literally the crux of the ancient, primordial instinct of the world centre, and why it could exist anywhere. 'Here' is always the centre; all the billions of human beings on this planet experience themselves perceptually at the centres of their worlds – the horizon seemingly encircles an individual, as if it were the circumference of a circle with the person at its centre. The psychologist Carl Gustav Jung identified an archetype of quaternity and commented on 'the centering process and a radial arrangement' of human perception.[5] But the search for the centre can go even deeper than the human body itself reaching down into the depths of the mind. The mysterious axis at the centre of the world was a feature of shamanism, for it is the passage between this and the spirit otherworlds or states of consciousness.

The three shamanic worlds

The basic shamanic model is of three worlds connected by a 'vertical' axis: the underworld of the ancestors, the middle world of human existence and the heavenworld, as reflected in the *axis mundi* symbol of Yggdrasil (see page 19), for instance. The shaman would 'journey' to the otherworlds in an out-of-body trance, flying to the World Tree, Cosmic Mountain or whatever other form in which the *axis mundi* was culturally envisaged. The shaman went 'down' or 'up' this to enter the underworld or heavenworld respectively.

The wooden frame of a Siberian shaman's drum was traditionally

ABOVE A shaman playing his drum in a ritual in Tuva, Siberia, Russia. The wooden frame of the drum is traditionally considered to be made from a branch of the World Tree.

considered to have been fashioned from a branch of the World Tree, an image of which might be painted on the drum's skin. The Goldi shaman's ceremonial robe even had a depiction of the World Tree emblazoned on it. The Siberian Chukchee shaman saw the pole (north) star as a hole in the sky through which access to the spirit worlds could be made. In trance, his spirit would float upwards with the smoke from the central fire through the smoke hole to the pole star.

The world centre at the intersection of the Four Directions is, then, the human mind – the crack between the worlds where access to the spiritual otherworlds can take place. Projected outwards beyond mind and body, the concept gave a people their physical, territorial bearings as well as locating them in symbolic space. It helped them to map time by measuring the rising and setting of sun, moon, stars and planets against an oriented and orderly segmented skyline. And it linked them back to mythic time, to the First People, and impregnated the landscape around them with meaning. The world centre was the core of much sacred cartography in the ancient world.

WALKING THROUGH HOLY LANDS
The Geography of Pilgrimage

*P*ilgrimages are journeys undertaken to particular places with the aim of inner, spiritual enhancement, healing, petitioning for divine assistance, simple worship or fulfilment of a religious duty. Pilgrimage destinations, like the motives for pilgrimage, can be highly varied. They can be long-venerated natural places such as mountains, caves, springs or waterfalls, or a place where a vision was experienced or where a deity or holy person (historical or mythical) performed some act. More often, the focus of a pilgrimage is a temple or shrine, perhaps containing the miracle-working relics of a saint.

The pilgrimage destination 'engages or disengages the senses, edifies the mind, and leads the soul back to the world of the spirit', author E. V. Walter remarks.[1] Put simply, a pilgrimage is the formal visit to a place that presents some tangible aspect of the sacred to the seeker.

The choreography of geography

The holy days of pilgrimage offer someone an opportunity for self-discovery through preparations for and expectations of the journey, the mental and physical rigours and experiences of the travelling itself, and the liberation from normal everyday life. This provides fertile mental ground for a spiritual interaction with the holy places visited and the landscape through which the designated pilgrimage route is taken, especially if it is a walking pilgrimage – in our era of rapid transportation, this aspect of pilgrimage can easily be overlooked.

ABOVE **Walking sticks with scallops – St. James' shell – the symbol of St. James and the Christian pilgrimage, displayed for sale as souvenirs on the way to the Cathedral of Santiago de Compostela, the final destination on the pilgrimage route.**

Sacred cartography

A pilgrimage route often provided a choreographed experience, though more so in the past than nowadays: a pilgrim would stop at a shrine here and there along the way, pass by locations associated with miracles and visions, stay at wayside accommodation for pilgrims and there

share beliefs and experiences with fellow pilgrims and, when finally nearing the end of the journey, would experience the thrill of the first glimpses of the pilgrimage's goal, be it a mountain peak, cathedral spire or gleaming temple dome. The geography of a pilgrimage journey can become a narrative, a holy text. Such sacred cartography can be writ large, involving whole landscapes or a town's layout; or small, involving a temple precinct or the architecture of a temple, requiring the pilgrim to process along a predetermined route.

The effect of a pilgrimage can often be carried back to the home of the pilgrim. 'Pilgrimage is as concerned with taking back some part of the charisma of a holy place as it is about actually going to the place,' pilgrimage scholars Simon Coleman and John Elsner observe.[2] For centuries pilgrimage-related industries have produced tokens such as small lead images of saints, plaques – or, nowadays, photographs – displaying images associated with a site, and containers of water or soil from a pilgrimage destination. These objects acted not only as mementoes for the pilgrim, but as promotion on behalf of the pilgrimage location. This is well instanced in the great European pilgrimage tradition associated

with St James of Compostela, Spain (see page 62), where scallop shells (both actual and manufactured) became the symbol of that pilgrimage shrine. Sometimes mementoes of one pilgrimage place become deposited at another shrine, thus creating subtle networks of sacred significance.

Early holy days

The act of pilgrimage seems to have been conducted as far back into human history as it is possible to see, and belongs to all faiths and creeds, both ancient and modern. We can suspect that pilgrimage occurred in prehistory, but we cannot now directly tell if that was so. But we do have hints.

Unexpected findings by archeologist Roy Loveday reveal the probable existence of a pilgrimage landscape in Stone Age Britain. Loveday was studying a distinctive group of Neolithic henge monuments (circular ditch-and-bank enclosures) in England: what made them a distinct type of henge was that they had two entrances, each opposite the other, giving the monuments axial orientations; and Loveday came up with the curious finding that these axes created by the opposing entrances had similar orientations with local stretches of Roman roads. He realized there could not be a direct connection between the Neolithic builders of the henges and the Roman road-makers more than 2,000 years later, but the relationship between such orientations occurred too frequently and was too widespread to be due to mere chance. Loveday concluded that the double-entrance henges were stations on pilgrimage routes. His theory is that the cultural significance attached to this pilgrimage landscape eventually declined,

RIGHT The temple of the Egyptian goddess Isis at Philae is one of many where inscribed foot markings are found. These markings are seen as evidence that Isis attracted a pilgrimage cult.

ABOVE Celtic pilgrimage routes are often marked with Celtic crosses.

the henges fell into disuse and all but disappeared from view, but the general courses of the routes linking them were found useful to later societies and so they survived in different contexts, the Roman roads being just one of the later ones. As Loveday commented, 'once a route has been established it is likely to endure'.[3]

An entirely other kind of clue regarding probable early pilgrimage activity comes from Greco-Roman times (an era spanning the latter centuries BCE and the early centuries CE). There is evidence that the Egyptian goddess Isis attracted a pilgrimage cult, built largely on her association with healing, and that she was celebrated with an annual festival. Her temples are found within larger religious complexes at locations around the Mediterranean, such as Abydos, Philae, Delos, Thessalonika, Rome and many others. Inscribed foot

markings are found at them – an apt symbol of the pilgrim. In numerous Isis temples inscribed foot-sole impressions (sometimes single, sometimes paired, sometimes shod, but often barefoot) are found with dedications such as 'to Isis the nymph', 'to Isis the fruit-bringer' or 'to Isis the queen', along with the name of the person dedicating the symbol. By piecing together the fragments representing these markings, Classics scholar Sarolta Takacs has worked out what seems to have been the basic choreographed route within the temple that the Isis pilgrim would have taken in the final approach to the shrine.[4]

Pre-Christian Celtic pilgrimages

Pilgrimages in Ireland are nowadays ostensibly Christian, but some of the oldest ones are almost certainly based on pre-Christian routes. It has been noted that many churches in mainland Ireland were founded on the borders of ancient kingdoms. Archeologist Nancy Edwards observes that pagan religious sanctuaries occupied similar positions. 'Some important churches were undoubtedly founded in places which had formerly been of pagan significance, and in certain cases pagan rites seem to have continued in a Christianized context,' she writes.[5]

It is also not difficult to suspect that Irish Christian pilgrimages to natural places had pre-Christian, pagan roots. An example is the pilgrimage route up to Mount Brandon on the Dingle peninsula in south-west Ireland. Archeologist Peter Harbison remarks upon the 'extreme likelihood of the mountain having been the focus of an ancient Lughnasa festival during the prehistoric Iron Age'.[6] According to myth, Mount Brandon was sacred to Lug, the pagan Celtic god of light, whose festival took place at the start of the harvest season: the end of July and the beginning of August. The peak was presumably Christianized by naming it after the 5th-century St Brendan. The remains of a path leading up towards the peak from the south coast of the peninsula are known as the Saint's Road and form one of two pilgrimage routes ascending the mountain. On the way are occasional stone pillars and natural rocks carved with ogham script (an ancient Celtic alphabet) and crosses shaped in the characteristic Celtic pilgrim fashion. Next to the marked boulders are small hollowed-out stones known as *bullauns* in which rainwater collects; it would have been considered holy water by pilgrims, perhaps even possessing healing powers. Also on the Saint's Road is the now-ruined 12th-century church at Kilmalkedar. This was dedicated to Maolcethair, a saint with a local cult that is known to have preceded that of St Brendan. In addition at this site there

is an oratory of drystone construction built in an ancient design of monks' cells, reminiscent in shape of the hull of an upturned boat. A similar, but better-preserved feature, the remarkable Gallarus Oratory, is set a short distance off the Saint's Road further along, just where the peak of Mount Brandon becomes visible over an intervening ridge.

ABOVE Some of the oldest pilgrimages in Ireland are based on pre-Christian routes. The church at Kilmalkedar, County Kerry was dedicated to a saint that is known to have pre-dated the Christian St Brendan.

Faithscapes: Hinduism

Hinduism has a great tradition of pilgrimage, and the Indian subcontinent can boast approximately 150 major centres that collectively draw about 20 million pilgrims annually, not to mention minor shrine sites. The act of travelling to or between pilgrimage sites is considered sacred in its own right, with the Vedas (Hindu sacred texts) stating that the pilgrim's sins are 'slain by the toil of his journeying'.

An Indian (Sanskrit) term for pilgrimage is *tirthayatra*; *yatra* relates to travelling, while *tirtha* means 'ford', a word that can mean a crossing place at a river or, more metaphorically, 'crossing over' – in the context of pilgrimage, this indicates passing from the mundane, secular world to the sacred. India's sacred rivers – the Ganges, Godavari, Yamuna, Narmada and others – can be thought of as '*tirtha* waters',[7] in that along their banks are holy 'crossings', combining in many cases both the physical and metaphorical sense of *tirtha*. The great pilgrimage centre of Varanasi (Benares) is the classic example of these.

There is a conception of the whole of India being a sacred landscape homogenized by pilgrimage routes. Pilgrims have circumambulated the whole of India, sometimes bringing water or sand from one holy place to another. Such linkages between pilgrimage sites throughout India are underpinned by myth. For example, one legend tells of a priest from Varanasi who cast his special cane into the well at Biraja, a pilgrimage site in Orissa. On returning to Varanasi, the priest found the cane floating in the Ganges.

The Braj faithscape

There are also very specific choreographed landscapes, 'faithscapes', at individual holy places. One of the best examples is at Braj, a region to the south of Delhi in Uttar Pradesh. It is a major pilgrimage centre dedicated to Lord Krishna, the Hindu god of love. The complex is in fact a cultural landscape consisting of a mixed woodland and pasture area with the sacred Yamuna River flowing through it. The ancient city of Mathura, which is associated with Jainism, Buddhism and Hinduism, is contained within the zone, as are other sacred centres and some 4,000 shrines. Mathura is regarded as the place where Krishna was born; in the Krishna myth, his father smuggled him out to the countryside to escape from a tyrant. There, Krishna became a cowherd and flirted with the milkmaids. He overcame demons in the forests, performed miracles and mischievously played tricks – called *lila*, or divine play. The Braj topography hosts virtually every event in the mythical life of Krishna.

The mythic association of Krishna with Mathura goes back to the 4th century CE, and there are hints of elements from an earlier animistic nature religion being absorbed into it – Krishna urging his contemporaries to worship a mountain rather than Indra, for instance. The sacred geography of Braj as it now is, though, was created only in the 16th century, when the Krishna pilgrimage was codified by the

OPPOSITE **Hindu pilgrims bathing at the *ghats* in the Ganges at Varanasi, India. Varanasi is the key pilgrimage destination for Hindus and is especially sacred to Shiva.**

poet-priest Narayan Bhatt. In laying down the itinerary of the pilgrimage, he focused on the groves in the landscape as the key devotional sites, and even Mathura became an honorary 'grove'. He catalogued them all, identifying Krishna-related myths with them and prescribing the rituals appropriate to them. Pilgrims flock to Braj during the August–September monsoon season, when the otherwise dry and dusty landscape is turned into lush greenery.

The pilgrimage circuit through Braj is essentially a joyful walk from grove to grove, starting and ending at Mathura.[8] At points along the circuit, various temples lay claim to specific parts of the Krishna mythos. For example, the 500-year-old Radha Raman Temple houses an image of fossilized stone, said to be inhabited by the god; he is awoken each day prior to sunrise by singing priests ringing bells and is bathed and dressed. Again, certain locales within the faithscape are where Krishna and his favourite consort, Radha, held their trysts, and there is one temple that pilgrims are not allowed to visit after dark, so as not to disturb Krishna and Radha in their love-making. A special aspect of the Braj faithscape is Ras Lila, a form of dance-drama in which events in the life of Krishna are played out in the landscape. They are spectacle and liturgy combined.

Varanasi

A mention of Varanasi has to be made when discussing faithscapes because it is the key pilgrimage destination for Hindus. It is especially sacred to Shiva, and is situated on the banks of the River Ganges. The holy city has more than 70 *ghats* (riverside shrines) consisting of platforms and stairs rising up from the water. Five specific *ghats* form a pilgrimage sequence, and pilgrims bathe at them in a fixed order. In all, though, Varanasi offers 56 pilgrimage circuits, forming a most complex sacred geography.

Buddhism and before

In Tibet, probably more than anywhere else, Buddhist influence fused most completely with the existing indigenous religion, which in the case of Tibet was the shamanic bon tradition. These earlier elements are welded inextricably with the form of Buddhism that replaced them. Tibetans refer to a sacred place as gnas *or* gnas-pa, *a location that is pervaded by the existing presence of a spirit, a god, a buddha or other supernatural force – an active residence of spiritual powers.*

ABOVE **Tibetan pilgrims on the pilgrimage around Mount Kailas. Pilgrims lie fully prostrate to enable the body to have contact with the spiritually cleansing powers in the sacred ground.**

Tibetans commonly use the term *gnas-skor* to refer to a pilgrimage centre, meaning 'going around a *gnas*', because a Tibetan pilgrimage is usually a circular journey. A characteristic of traditional Tibetan pilgrimage is the performing of full-length body prostrations. This enables the body to have full contact with the sacred ground, with the spiritually cleansing powers residing there.

Mount Kailas

A classic instance of this takes place around Mount Kailas in the Himalayas. From a standing position with the hands held together in prayer, a Tibetan pilgrim will kneel, bow down, then lie full-length on the ground, touching it with his or her forehead. Pilgrims then mark a spot with the nose, rise again and walk to that spot, then repeat the whole cycle. And so they proceed around the mountain.

A 50-km (32-mile) pilgrims' path around Kailas at an altitude of about 4,877 metres (16,000 feet) was erased during the Chinese Cultural Revolution and has not been rebuilt, but some of the shrine sites that marked the route and were also destroyed have had their locations indicated by rocks and boulders. A fit, walking pilgrim can get round the Kailas circuit in one or two days, but those using the prostration method may take up to two weeks.

Mount Fuji

In Japan, mountain pilgrimage was one of the first kinds of Buddhist expression to emerge out of earlier indigenous Shinto and folk religious beliefs. In the 8th century CE Buddhism in Japan developed the 'Nature Wisdom School', which encouraged the search for spiritual enlightenment by being close to nature in the mountains. The indigenous shamans who had developed their powers through mountain asceticism became loosely associated with this, and there emerged Shugen-do, the Order of

Mountain Ascetics. The Shinto *kami*, or spirits of the mountains, were translated into Buddhist divinities.

A few centuries later, mountain pilgrimage became very popular, and by the end of the 19th century it was estimated that there were 17,000 guides leading pilgrims to sacred mountain peaks, which indicates the scale of such pilgrimage – at least partially a function of the fact that much of Japan is composed of mountainous terrain with a multiplicity of sacred peaks. Even today, the country boasts many dozens of major pilgrimage circuits.

The great mountain of Japan is, of course, Mount Fuji. It was – and is – regarded as a sacred peak, dedicated by Buddhists to the Bodhisattva of Wisdom and by the Shinto religion to Konohana Sakuya Hime, the goddess of flowering trees. There was an established pilgrims' way up the mountainside as early as the 14th century, and over the following centuries many people have claimed visionary experiences on Mount Fuji. Pilgrims still flock there, with hundreds of thousands wending their way up the mountainside during the key period of July and August. Straw models of the mountain are burned as part of a fire ritual, an association with the volcanic nature of the mountain, and a lacquered model weighing more than 1 tonne (1 ton) is carried to the summit. The pilgrimage route has ten stations, at each of which a character is branded into the pilgrim's walking stick or staff. At the top, which is ideally reached at dawn, the pilgrim circumambulates the crater rim.

The Ajanta caves

Buddhists in India tended to extend an earlier tradition of the religious use of caves. Probably the best-known Indian Buddhist cave shrine is Ajanta – a richly painted rock-hewn temple complex in a bend of the Waghora River in the Deccan. The Ajanta caves were created between 200 BCE and 650 CE. Although no longer an official pilgrimage destination, people still come here to leave flowers and incense. Another cave pilgrimage complex is Kanheri, near Mumbai (Bombay), which was like Ajanta, but continued as an active centre for longer. Hundreds of caves were carved out of rock and natural caverns were enlarged nearly 2,000 years ago, containing steps, rooms, carvings and pilgrims' inscriptions.

The Pagan complex

In Myanmar (Burma), as elsewhere, Buddhism merged with the earlier earth religions. An interesting circular example of this is the complex at Pagan, where the 1,000-year-old ruins of a multitude of temples and stupas stretch for 13 km (8 miles) along the River Irrawaddy. Buddhist observances are still made at a few of them, although the true Buddhist tradition has all but disappeared. Ironically, the nature religion that preceded Buddhism has crept back, for sprinkled among the temples are wooden shrines, seen as spirit houses. Some Burmese Buddhists observe this nature religion alongside their Buddhism, and the Gawdawpalin Temple at Pagan is an ancestor shrine, where pilgrims still come to honour their ancestors.

ABOVE **Buddhism has merged with earlier earth religions in Myanmar. The temple complex at Pagan includes wooden shrines, seen as spirit houses**

Onward, Christian pilgrims

One of the earliest of the great Christian pilgrimages was to Mount Sinai in Egypt, the Horeb of biblical record, where Moses saw the burning bush and received the tablets of the law. It was established by the 4th century CE, *reaching its climax about 200 years later, when the entire area was marked with significant spots where the pilgrim might pause to pray.*

ABOVE **The Christian pilgrimage to Mount Sinai is a sacred journey through the landscape, during which the pilgrims perform various ritual activities.**

This pilgrimage destination, with the monastery of St Catherine at its centre, became a form of 'theology fixed in space', as scholars Simon Coleman and John Elsner put it – pilgrims traced 'a biblical narrative through the landscape'.[9] They visited mythologized places such as the rock where Moses struck water, the site of the burning bush, the spring where Moses watered sheep, the cave where Elijah fled from King Ahab and the peak of Mount Sinai itself, where a small church marked the spot on which Moses is said to have received the tablets of the law. A series of prayer niches existed on the pilgrimage route up the mountain. Coleman and Elsner remark that these were located at 'places where the path joined another path, or places where pilgrims might glimpse a view of the distant peak (their goal)'. The pilgrims performed various ritual activities on their sacred journey through the landscape, such as hymn-singing, praying, cross-carrying and hair-cutting with which to make offerings.

Iona

The small island of Iona, off the west coast of the Scottish Highlands, was an early British Christian pilgrimage target. St Columba arrived on the island from Ireland in the 6th century with a small band of monastic followers. The island possesses a natural wild beauty, fostering an almost tangible mystical mood, which even today visitors often remark upon, and it might well have been considered holy in pagan times, long before Columba set foot on it. It served as the saint's monastic base, from where he set out on periodic missions to convert the pagan peoples of Scotland. By the time this great Celtic Christian saint died in 597, Iona's fame had become widespread. Despite a dip in its influence during a lengthy period of Viking raids (in one of which monks were massacred), its sanctity continued to be recognized, and between the 8th and 11th centuries Scottish, Norse and Irish kings were interred in the burial ground of Reilig Odhrain there. Around 1200 CE, a Benedictine abbey was built on the remains of earlier churches, and a tiny cell shrine by the west end of the abbey probably marks the position of Columba's grave. After the Reformation in the 16th century the abbey and its satellite buildings fell into decay.

Little is now known about the early pilgrimage tradition at Iona – there seems to have been a guest-house, and the provision of hospitality was said to be a feature of the Columbine community. Visits were seemingly limited to specific times, and then for only a fixed number of days. The island's sacred geography was apparently mapped on the life and actions of Columba, and modern scholars have tried to reconstruct this. Places featuring in

the cartography include a still-visible banked ditch that encircled the original monastic community; Cnoc an t-Sithean, the hill where St Columba was seen to discourse with the shimmering white forms of angels, and the Bay of Coracles where Columba first landed. There is also little doubt that Columba's huts would have been seen as shrines, in addition to which well over 300 crosses that were erected around the island, though most were destroyed at the Reformation. Fortunately, the fine 9th-century St Martin's cross survives intact, and some others were restored. From the harbour on Iona a road called Sraid nam Marbh, the Street of the Dead, runs to the Reilig Odhrain burial ground, and then goes on to the monastery and Columba's shrine. 'This cobbled road was the grand processional route use by funerals and pilgrims, marked by a trail of ornamental crosses, chapels and burial grounds, with side-paths leading off directing pilgrims towards some of the satellite sites,' Scottish archeologist Peter Yeoman informs us.[10]

Jerusalem

The most prized destination for early Christian pilgrimage was Jerusalem, and between the 4th and 7th centuries there was an attempt to create a Christianized spiritual geography within the city. More than 300 churches were built and two Constantine basilicas – the Eleona Church on the Mount of Olives, and the Church of the Holy Sepulchre on the Hill of Golgotha, the site of the crucifixion and resurrection –

together with the Church of the Nativity in nearby Bethlehem.[11]

The various sites were conceptually linked in the form of a liturgy developed by Cyril, the Bishop of Jerusalem between 349 and 386. This involved movement from one church to another, with scriptural readings and prayers relating to the New Testament significance of each site being recited at that place at the appropriate time. Pilgrims saw and touched the places where they believed Christ had been present, and this sometimes led to reported visions. The most celebrated visionary of this kind was St Helena, who had a vision on Golgotha that led her to the place where the True Cross, the cross of the crucifixion, had been buried. It is claimed that she validated it by raising a dead person at the spot.

ABOVE The Island of Iona off the Scottish Highlands has a natural beauty that has drawn visitors for centuries.

LEFT *St. Helena and the Miracle of the True Cross* (oil on canvas), Simon Marmion (fl.1450-89). Saint Helena had a vision that led her to the true cross of the crucifixion. According to Christian tradition, the authenticity of the cross was verified when a human corpse placed in contact with it was restored to life.

Santiago de Compostela

The greatest Christian pilgrimage in medieval Europe was the journey to the church of St James of Compostela (Santiago de Compostela) in Galicia, north-west Spain, believed to contain the tomb of the apostle St James the Greater. It was thought that after the saint's martyrdom in Jerusalem in 44 CE, the body was miraculously transported to Galicia, where it was unearthed in the 9th century by a farmer or hermit who was led to it by a mysterious star.

At the pilgrimage's peak of popularity, multitudes were drawn to the church because of the claims of miracles. Routes led to Santiago from all over Europe, all meeting at Puente La Reina, the starting point of El Camino de Santiago, the pilgrims' way that cuts east–west across northern Spain through Burgos, Leon and Astorga. It crosses two mountain ranges and an arid plain, but there were hospices spaced along it, each a day's walk apart. Shrines were also placed along the route, marking holy or significant places such as monasteries and convents, caves uses by anchorites, places where holy people had been born or died, reliquaries and the sites of miracles and wonders. Most pilgrims wanted to gain promised remission of their sins by arriving on the main feast day, 25 July. When the pilgrims reached the cathedral, they entered by the west doorway, the Portico de la Gloria, dating to 1168. Then, as now, they touched the central pillar of the doorway, worn smooth

by countless such contacts. At the high altar, on which the jewel-encrusted statue-shrine of St James is situated, the pilgrims climbed up steps to reach through an open space and kiss the effigy's neck.

Canterbury

No discussion of medieval pilgrimage can be made without a reference to the English one to Canterbury Cathedral in Kent. In medieval times it ranked as one of the chief pilgrimage destinations in western Europe.

St Augustine founded the original cathedral in the 6th century on the site of an earlier church. The oldest part of the present cathedral, though, is the crypt, dating to 1100. St Thomas à Becket was murdered in the cathedral in 1170, at the hands of four knights of King Henry II's court. Thomas was immediately recognized as a martyr; reports at the time state that people came while his body still lay in the cathedral, collecting his spilled blood and taking shreds of his clothing, which they dipped in the blood. Miracles began to be claimed at once – a paralysed woman who was smeared with

a piece of bloodied clothing was healed on the night of the murder, and 20 more cures were reported in the following weeks. Within a year pilgrims from all across Europe and the British Isles were descending on Canterbury, and by 1173 Thomas was canonized. Reports of miracles continued, and there was a brisk trade in phials of 'Canterbury Water', in which a droplet of the martyr's blood was supposedly dissolved. Accounts of the time describe the bejewelled and gold-plated shrine as breathtaking.

In southern England, several pilgrimage routes to Canterbury were created, but there were two primary ones. One, commencing in Southwark, London, was the route followed by Chaucer's fictional (or fictionalized) band of pilgrims in his *Canterbury Tales*. The other, a 160-km (100-mile) route still known as the Pilgrim's Way and marked for parts of its length on modern maps, commences at Winchester. From there the Way runs north through many villages and also through an Iron Age earthwork called Bigbury hillfort. The original track no longer exists in its entirety, but sections survive. Indeed, some segments of the Way may have preceded Christianity – in his *The Old Road* (1904), Hilaire Belloc argued that the route was in fact an updating of a major east–west prehistoric ridgeway route through southern England, probably providing access to the great ceremonial centres of Salisbury Plain, where Stonehenge is located. Similar to many pilgrimage routes, the Pilgrim's Way acts like a kind of time machine that occupies a ribbon of space.

When they reached Canterbury Cathedral, pilgrims were obliged to follow a specific route through the building, acknowledging various stations, such as the spot where the saint had been killed and the high altar where the body had been laid. When they reached the shrine, pilgrims ircumambulated it barefoot or on their knees. Because he viewed Thomas as having been a traitor, and was suspicious of the power base that

Canterbury Cathedral had become, Henry VIII had everything within the cathedral removed or destroyed. So it is that today there is an empty space where the shrine once stood, and a modern monument marks where the saint was martyred. But the time-worn steps eloquently stand witness to the power of pilgrims' feet.

Walsingham

Another great English pilgrimage destination was Walsingham, Norfolk, where a vision of the Virgin was said to have shown Lady Richeldis de Faverches the holy house in Nazareth, where – according to the Christian mythos – the angel Gabriel announced the Annunciation and where Jesus dwelt as a child.

Two springs gushed forth at the location of the vision (though these may have been existing pagan wells). The lady of the manor constructed a copy of the holy house to the instructions given to her in the vision. The wooden structure was succeeded by a series of stone buildings. During the 13th century, royalty made devotional journeys to Walsingham, and the pilgrimage tradition became internationally famous. Various relics were gathered at the shrine, including the supposed milk of the Virgin, fragments of the True Cross and a wooden statue of the Madonna and Child, which became associated with miracle cures. Henry VIII eventually suppressed this pilgrimage destination as well, burning the statue. The tradition was revived in the 20th century as a multi-denominational Christian pilgrimage.

ABOVE The tradition of pilgrimage to Walsingham in Norfolk, England, was suppressed under the rule of King Henry VIII but was revived in the 20th century.

The Hajj

Probably the most universally known pilgrimage is the Hajj, the devotional journey to Mecca, Saudi Arabia, the birthplace of Mohammed and centre of the Islamic faith. Muslims are supposed to perform the pilgrimage at least once in their lifetimes, circumstances permitting.

ABOVE Pilgrims perform a *tawaf,* **the anticlockwise circumambulation of the Ka'ba seven times. Prayers are recited and attempts are made to touch or kiss the Black Stone in the eastern corner.**

The Hajj is the fifth Pillar of Islam – the five duties incumbent on every Muslim in order that they live a good and responsible life. It takes place once a year in the month of Dhul Hijjah, the twelfth month of the Islamic lunar calendar. The Hajj sees almost 3 million Muslims of every ethnic group, social class and culture gather together every year, promoting the bonds of brotherhood in order to show that everyone is equal in the eyes of Allah.

The pilgrimage destination has a tightly mapped sacred geography. The central focus is the Ka'ba, a huge cuboid shrine located in the centre of the largest mosque in the world, the Masjid al-Harram in the city of Mecca. The pilgrims have to undergo a purification process before entering the al-Harram mosque, home of the Ka'ba. The state of ritual purity pilgrims attain is called *Ihram*. After abstaining from indulgence of the physical senses, donning a special white garment, also called *Ihram*, and men having their hair cut, the threshold of the temple is crossed barefoot, right foot first. The initial part of the pilgrimage circuit involves the *tawaf*, the anticlockwise circumambulation of the Ka'ba seven times. Specific prayers are recited at each corner of the structure, and the sacred, probably meteoric Black Stone that is lodged in the eastern corner is gestured to, touched or even kissed, if the press of pilgrims allows. Afterwards, pilgrims proceed to a causeway linking two small hills, now simply slight elevations, al-Safwa and al-Marwa, along which they run back and forth seven times. This action honours a search for water by Hajar, wife of the Prophet Abraham. At a later point the pilgrims visit the holy places of Jabal ar-Rahma, Mujdalifah and Mina, in the desert around Mecca, ending up at the Mount of Mercy at Arafat, where sermons are heard and prayers said. The following day, on the route back towards Mecca, pilgrims stop at Mina, and over a period of three days throw a set number of stones at three 25-metre (82-foot)-high stone pillars called Jamaraat, said to mark the place where Abraham rejected the devil by throwing stones at him. Pilgrims then sacrifice an animal, usually a sheep or goat, in commemoration of God accepting as sacrifice a sheep instead of the Prophet Abraham's son. Pilgrims then return to Mecca and the al-Harram Mosque to perform another *tawaf*.

BELOW Hajj pilgrims gather at the Mount of Mercy at Arafat to say prayers. The hill is the place Muslims believe the Prophet Mohammad gave his farewell sermon.

Sacred journeying in the ancient Americas

Pilgrimage was a factor in Native American life as well, though we will probably never know the full extent of it. What relatively little we can determine derives from clues to be found in ethnology, a few traditions that still survive and archeological evidence.

ABOVE Shamanic rock art in Grapevine Canyon. The engravings of bighorn sheep are the signatures of rain shamans, some of whom travelled hundreds of miles to this place.

'Zuni Heaven'

Every four years a group of Zunis from Arizona still make a pilgrimage of more than 160 km (100 miles) to 'Zuni Heaven', retracing part of the course of the mythic migratory route from their point of origin (see page 45). The group of usually up to 60 tribal members makes offerings, recites prayers and gathers natural materials for making ceremonial paint pigments. 'The Zuni trail itself is sacred, with every geologic and natural feature having special meaning,' states historian Andrew Gulliford.[12] It is a strenuous journey and takes four days to complete. We do not know how old this pilgrimage tradition might be, but we do have Spanish records informing us that in 1570 CE Francisco Vasquez de Coronado encountered Zuni priests making this solemn journey.

Grapevine Canyon

A little to the west there is fragmentary ethnology and some archeological evidence telling of a pre-Columbian pilgrimage route used possibly by Yuman tribespeople. It seems to have started from a point at or near Pilot Knob, a modest peak near Winterhaven in southern California, close to the border with Mexico.

The pilgrimage route went northwards along the Colorado River valley. Scattered along this north–south corridor there are giant human and animal figures etched into the desert ground, as will be described later (see page 94). Alongside some of these huge desert markings, researchers have detected circular areas of compacted earth, suggesting that they were dance grounds. It seems highly probable that these points were ritual stations on the route. The destination of the 240-km (150-mile)-long pilgrimage seems to have been Grapevine Canyon (see page 82), at the foot of a bare stone peak located just within the southern tip of Nevada, known by several modern names including, aptly, Dead Mountain. Its native name is Avikwa'ame, 'Spirit Mountain'. Grapevine Canyon is known to have been considered the 'house' of the creator being, Mastamho. It was resorted to by tribal shamans from hundreds of kilometres around in order to seek visions there.[13] The record of those visions (at least some of which were powered by mind-altering plants, such as the datura-containing jimson weed) can be found in hundreds, if not thousands, of rock engravings that grace the canyon's walls.

Elsewhere in California, the Karuk people still perform their pilgrimage, though its course alongside the Klamath River has been decimated by modern obstructions. However, local authorities

agreed to erect 'Ritual Crossing' signs at the point where the Karuk celebrants needed to cross a highway.

Cholula and Wirikutá

Moving south into Mexico, one of the chief deities of the Aztecs was Quetzalcoatl, the feathered or plumed serpent, a mythic image much older than the Aztec civilization. They believed the divinity lived at Cholula, south of present-day Mexico City. Cholula is greatly ruined, but still has its huge pyramid, even though that now looks more like an earthen hill and is topped with a church. Although founded many hundreds of years earlier, Cholula was made the pilgrimage centre for their Quetzalcoatl cult by the Aztecs.

Another exceptionally ancient pilgrimage in Mexico is still observed by the Huichol people. They undertake an annual sacred journey of several hundred kilometres from their mountain homeland to a high plateau region called Wirikutá, considered their land of origin. A shaman-priest, the *mara'akame*, leads the pilgrims. The Huichol consider that they are retracing

ABOVE The Karuk people in California still perform their pilgrimage alongside the Klamath River.

ABOVE **The Huichol people of Mexico undertake a sacred journey to Wirikutá every year, retracing the steps of the First People to their land of origin.**

RIGHT **One of the chief deities of the Aztecs was Quetzalcoatl, the feathered or plumed serpent. The Aztecs made Cholula the pilgrimage centre for their Quetzalcoatl cult.**

the steps of the First People, and at specific locations they perform various actions attributed to those mythic ancestors. At Wirikutá a hunt for, and ritual consumption of, the hallucinogenic peyote cactus takes place. The cactus is referred to as a 'deer' and the first one found is ritually shot with an arrow – some anthropologists think this whole pilgrimage could be a vestige of an extremely archaic tradition of the Great Hunt, brought over the Beringia land bridge from Siberia. The peyote deer-hunt at Wirikutá is the peak experience in the religious life of the Huichol. Baskets of the cactus are gathered and taken back as sacramental hallucinogens for use in religious activities.

Chavin de Huantar and Cahuachi

South America also offers fragmentary evidence of major pilgrimage activity. The Peruvian temple of Chavin de Huantar, a strange structure well over 2,000 years old, was the main centre and oracle for a cult that covered a vast Andean area and had plant hallucinogens, especially the mind-altering San Pedro cactus, as its sacraments. Pilgrims bearing offerings and wishing to consult the oracle came from throughout the Andean region. They had to move around the temple complex along a route predetermined by the architecture of the place, though the exact pattern of movement is not fully understood by archeologists. The oracle 'spoke' by means of a roaring sound created by the opening and closing of gates in a curiously over-engineered drainage system.

Further south along the Peruvian Andes is Cahuachi, near the famed Nazca Lines. Dating from between 1,500 and 2,000 years ago, Cahuachi is a complex of now almost destroyed temple building, mounds and pyramids, six of which were giant natural mounds that had adobe facings placed on their slopes. Some archeologists think the Nazca Lines were used by pilgrims as ritual ways, an idea to which we will return (see page 72).

Tiahuanaco

On the high Andean plain in Bolivia, the ancient and now-ruinous ceremonial city of Tiahuanaco, situated next to Lake Titicaca, flourished for almost a thousand years as a pilgrimage centre. It seems to have developed out of a religion that dominated the Titicaca basin as early as 1000 BCE, and there is evidence that the site of Tihuanaco was occupied by at least that date. But the city proper existed from c. 250 BCE. It was a planned holy city, with the architecture of its central core designed for public ceremony. Its main shrine was the Akapana, a great artificial, terraced hill faced in stone. As with Chavin de Huantar, this structure has an over-engineered drainage system, enabling it to make dramatic sound effects. At its height, Tiahuanaco's population may have numbered some 40,000 people, but this would naturally have increased at times of pilgrimage. Tiahauanaco's influence was extensive (again like Chavin de Huantar), so pilgrims must have come from long distances. Here, too, the ritual taking of mind-altering substances seems to have been at the heart of the tradition – at various points around the city archeologists have uncovered snuff trays, inhalation tubes and other paraphernalia well understood to have been used for the taking of psychoactive drugs. Tiahuanaco archeologist Alan Kolata has commented: 'Tiahuanaco became the ultimate centre of pilgrimage, an Andean Mecca, the first truly cosmopolitan city of the ancient Andean world.'[14]

There were a great many more pilgrimage centres throughout the Americas, some known, some still coming to light through archeological investigation, and others that will be lost to us for ever. But it is already clear that the urge to make choreographed journeys through lands and places invested with sanctity and mythological meaning was as much a worldwide phenomenon in the remotest past as it is now. Pilgrimage is another example of how landscape and the human mind became profoundly entwined from when history began.

LEFT **Carvings in the Peruvian temple of Chavin de Huantar show evidence of the use of the San Pedro cactus as a sacramental plant hallucinogen.**

LINES DRAWN IN THE LAND
The Secrets of Straightness

*T*he most direct form of ancient sacred geography was that which was mapped directly on the ground. Straight lines and ritual roads, patterns, images and effigies were etched into the land or built upon it, often on a large scale, by various cultures. They are the most mysterious of all sacred geographies because they relate to the inner beliefs and myths of peoples long gone. They are also now generally elusive, because by their nature they have become obscured by changing land use, weather conditions and belief systems, compounded by the fact that their scale in some instances rendered them invisible to later occupants of the landscapes involved.

The most enigmatic of these ground markings or 'geoglyphs' are those that appear at first glance to be simply lines – typically dead-straight lines. Most of the best examples are to be found in remote, wild and usually arid regions of the Americas, though some are discernible elsewhere, as we shall discover.

Mysterious straightness

*The Nasca Lines[1] in Peru are undoubtedly the most widely known example of straight-line ground markings. They occur on a 48-km (30-mile) stretch of desert tableland or **pampa** between Nasca and Palpa, on the western, coastal side of the Andes mountain range. They are referred to as 'intaglios' by archeologists because they are literally etched into the ground – the desert pavement topsoil, darkened by endless ages of oxidization, was removed, revealing a bright-yellowish sub-surface.*

ABOVE **The Nasca Lines in Peru are etched directly into the ground. Lines of up to 10 km (6 miles) long meet at ray centres or trapezoid areas.**

The Nasca Lines

Ruler-straight, these lines extend for up to 10 km (6 miles), are of varying widths and in some places run in close parallel groups, while in others they are solitary lines crossing the expanse of the tableland. The overall criss-crossing of the lines initially appears to form a random pattern, but there is an order of a kind embedded within the linear mesh. Lines meet or diverge at more than 60 'ray', 'line' or 'star-like' centres (as they are variously called), and at least one line from each links with another. In addition, there are also large trapezoid areas to which the straight lines connect in various ways. The linear markings are thought to date to the Nasca culture of *c.* 600 CE. They share the *pampa* with other kinds of (probably older) figurative and abstract intaglio markings.

Other Andean and Amazonian networks

Despite their fame, the Nasca Lines represent only one example of such features along the Andean cordillera. For a start, there are lines on other coastal pampas in that part of the Andes. And, far to the south of Nasca, there are straight lines in the Atacama Desert around Pintados in northern Chile, as well as figurative geoglyphs.[2] In Bolivia there are networks of straight pathways on the high Andean plain, the *altiplano*. The paths here are mainly formed by the clearance of vegetation and rocks along an exact straight course, punctuated by shrines. Some of these Bolivian lines extend to 32 km (20 miles) in length, longer than any of those at Nasca.

East of the Andes, researchers are finding mainly straight causeways and linear structures in various parts of the Amazon forest. The straightness cannot be explained away simply, as field archeologist William Denevan points out:

> *While the engineering needed to maintain a straight road in flat open terrain is relatively simple, building a long straight road to a destination that cannot be seen is not easy... Most of the stone causeways are on well-drained ground where a wide, well-beaten pathway would suffice. The raised, permanent road, then, takes on other significance.*[3]

Mayan causeways

Moving northwards in the Americas, the apparent obsessive straightness of such linear features is encountered again in Mexico as Mayan causeways. Known as *sacbeob* ('white ways') in the Mayan

language, these features in their prime ran as straight as an arrow and as flat as a rule through the Yucatán jungle, linking ancient Mayan ceremonial cities – the longest currently discovered runs for about 96 km (60 miles) between the ancient Mayan sites of Coba and Yaxuna in the northern Yucatán, though most of it now is in ruinous form.

The causeways also ran between features within the cities. They may have been roads, but they were also sacred ways, with altars stationed along them. One of their main archeological investigators, William Folan, emphasizes that such special types of road were often multi-functional in the Americas, allowing movement for both sacred and secular purposes. That the Mayan causeways had a deeper meaning is indicated in Mayan lore to this day, which tells of mythological underground *sacbeob*, supposedly linking the ritual Mayan ball-courts to be found in the ancient ceremonial cities, and invisible ones that run through the air, called Kusan Sum. One such virtual aerial route is said to run between the ancient Mayan cities of Dzibilchaltan and Izamal. There was an invisible network of straight ways.

ABOVE **Mayan causeways ran straight and flat through the Yucatán jungle, linking ceremonial cities. Altars placed along them suggest they were both roads and sacred ways.**

ASTRONOMICAL GUIDANCE?

There may have been even more linear patterning invisibly embedded in Anasazi sacred geography – invisible because it was on a very large scale. Archeologist Stephen Lekson has argued that there were three major Anasazi ceremonial centres, occupied and used sequentially from north to south over the centuries, starting with Aztec, about 96 km (60 miles) north of Chaco, then the canyon itself, and finally Paquime (Casas Grandes) in what is today northern Mexico.[6] Lekson further noted that these three Anasazi ceremonial capitals fall on an exact meridian, or north–south line (see map right), almost 725 km (450 miles) long, a feat that he thinks was achieved by means of astronomical knowledge, which it is widely agreed the Anasazi possessed. Yet again, the obsession with straightness is in evidence.

OPPOSITE LEFT One of the Great Kivas on the floor of Chaco Canyon. These were semi-subterranean chambers used for ceremonial and ritual activities.

OPPOSITE RIGHT NASA aerial photography has helped to reveal the extent of the Chacoan road system, which runs from Paquimé in northwestern Mexico to Aztec in New Mexico.

RIGHT Ceremonial stairway descending the north wall of Chaco Canyon. The Ansazi ceremonial roads on the surrounding desert met the tops of stairways like these, scattered throughout the canyon.

Mexican systems

Further northwards in Mexico there are several straight-road systems, such as the one around the citadel of La Quemada in Zacatecas, northern Mexico. This ceremonial complex, used by the Chalchihuites people between *c.* 600 and 800 CE, is built on a rocky hill that rises in solitary grandeur above the flat floor of the Malpaso Valley. The remnants of dead-straight stone roads criss-cross the valley floor all around the citadel, though now they are ruinous and barely discernible beneath the modern cover of vegetation. First studied by engineers in the 19th century, these slightly raised paved causeways were found to have altar-like features on them and to link ceremonial areas or run to natural features such as caves. American archeologist Charles Trombold, who has made a special investigation of La Quemada, comments that the causeways cannot be treated as ordinary roads, but rather that they had to be associated with ritual activities. He observes that these must have been important because the causeways represent considerable planning and organizational effort.[4]

Chacoan ceremonial roads

Similar linear phenomena appear in North America, too. The best example is probably the network of ceremonial roads around the Anasazi ritual centre of Chaco Canyon, south of Farmington in New Mexico. The Anasazi culture was at its peak *c.* 900–*c.* 1200 CE, and it seems to have evaporated during the 15th century for reasons unknown – though exceptional drought conditions and politico-religious upheavals have been suggested.

The canyon is a shallow rift with vertical rocky sides in high desert country and contains the ruins of 'Great Houses', thought to have been ceremonial rather than domestic buildings, along with numerous Great Kivas, semi-subterranean circular chambers used for ceremonial and ritual activities. The roads converge on the canyon, and are engineered features up to 10 metres (32 feet) wide, a fact made more remarkable because the Anasazi had neither beasts of burden nor wheeled

vehicles. NASA infrared aerial photography has further revealed that some sections of road have up to two parallel sections running alongside them, like modern multi-lane highways. The roads pass through or alongside some Great Houses situated out in the desert country surrounding the canyon, and their architecture appears to have been designed to accommodate them. The roads stop at the canyon rim, where steep, almost certainly ceremonial stairways cut into the canyon's walls descend to its floor.

Some Chacoan roads are known to extend for tens of kilometres, and perhaps even further – remnants of Anasazi roads have been found in all the Four Corner states of Utah, Arizona, Colorado and New Mexico. It is thought that the road system may have linked the major *kivas* in the Anasazi religious centres scattered across the 645-km (400-mile) breadth of the San Juan Basin, the Anasazi territory. It may well have been that the roads served multiple purposes, including mundane

transport, but there can be no doubt that religious activity was one of them. Animal sculptures have been found on some of the roads, as well as shrines and pottery fragments indicating ceremonial breakage, a common ritual practice in many ancient cultures. 'The most common feature of the Chaco roads is their straight line course which is maintained in spite of topographic obstacles,' states NASA archeologist Thomas Sever, who has made a special study of the features. 'The purpose for the straightness is not entirely clear and has never been satisfactorily answered.'[5] He noted that the Anasazi road-makers were not efficient in any modern sense, deliberately taking their roads straight through or over topographical obstacles.

There are numerous other examples of straight roads and tracks in the Americas, such as the Miwok trails in the California sierras, said to be 'airline-straight' in their directness, and 1,000-year-old straight pathways linking cemeteries in Costa Rica, to name just two.

Otherworld roads?

All these features are haunted by the mystery of what was clearly a deliberate concern with straightness. No one has fully solved this yet, even though it was obviously one of the common factors in the sacred geographies of different cultures throughout the Americas and spanning centuries or even millennia.

RIGHT **Historical image of Inca royalty on the road. Lower-class travellers would travel on a separate, parallel road.**

Trombold correctly observes, 'if there is one attribute that characterizes New World road systems, it is straightness.' The Navajo came to live in the Chaco region after it was vacated by the Anasazi, and one of their elders enigmatically told an archeologist in the 1920s that Chacoan roads may 'look like roads, but they are not roads'.[7] So what were they?

Symbolic associations

There is no doubt that many of the Native American linear features were multi-purpose, and it is unlikely there is one tidy, single explanation for any of them, as much as our modern, Westernized minds would like there to be. But as the great investigator of ancient Andean road systems, the late John Hyslop, correctly pointed out, roads constructed in the extraordinary ways we find in the ancient Americas probably reflect ritual or symbolic concerns. 'Attempts to interpret all aspects of prehistoric roads in purely materialist terms are bound to fail,' he warned.[8]

We can get hints of the deeper essence of the strange straightness from a number of disparate clues. We can start by dissecting the nature of the Nasca Lines and, by implication, perhaps other similar features.

Astronomical and social theories

Various explanations for the linear ground markings on the Nasca *pampa* have been proffered. Astronomical notions have been put forward, but these can at best be only partially explanatory, with many of the earlier astronomical theories being found wanting, as archeoastronomer and long-time Nasca Lines investigator, Anthony Aveni, has discovered.[9] There may have been a few alignments to celestial bodies by some of the lines, but it is now known that the Nasca *pampa* is far from being an

'astronomical blackboard' as used to be claimed. Another suggestion has been that the lines relate to places of burial on the *pampa*, but that remains less than convincing and in any case hardly accounts for the complexity of the markings.

More substantially, social explanations have also been proposed as a result of many years of historical and ethnological study of indigenous Andean societies. It is known, for instance, that in the past the Inca king and his entourage would travel along a central, straight Inca road, while lower-class travellers would use parallel roads, and that the Inca roads themselves were partially based on even earlier straight-road systems. And powerful class and kinship or clan structures continue to exist in today's Andean societies. These can be expressed in various forms of territorial management, such as when common, mundane spaces like village squares are being prepared for religious festivals: parallel strips of the area are ritually swept, each strip being the responsibility of a specific kinship group. Other linear devices are found in the division of land, whether for agricultural, social or religious purposes. Though such practices almost certainly derive from much earlier ones, it is not entirely clear exactly how they relate to features like the Nasca Lines. Nevertheless, there is evidence that some of the Nasca Lines were ritually swept in antiquity, and many researchers now consider that the *pampa area*, the wilderness beyond the inhabited valleys, was subject to various forms of social division – class, labour, ceremonial, religious – reflected in the linear networks. Yet even if this were so, it doesn't seem to quite reach the root of the linear mystery.

Water connections

A hydrological association with the lines is another explanatory approach. The provision of water to the arid coastal strip on the western side of the Andes is of prime concern to its inhabitants, now as it was in the past. It hardly ever rains there, and water comes down from the mountains as rivulets and streams, not from the sky overhead. It has therefore been proposed that the Nasca Lines point towards the sacred, water-giving mountains – the mountain gods and gods that were mountains, as the Inca believed. Yet a survey of several dozen *pampa* lines in the vicinity of the great sand mountain of Cerro Blanco, key in the rain rituals of the Nascans, failed to show a single one aligning to it.[10]

Spanish conquerors. Those who favour a water-related explanation of the Nasca Lines argue that they were used for rituals associated with the petitioning of the rain gods, as well as for mapping out the local water resources.

All these differing explanations seemingly make strange bedfellows, as Aveni admits, but he wisely counsels that 'there is a place for all these human actions and concepts in the story of the Nasca lines'. One explanation need not rule out the others. But if we probe carefully, all of them ultimately represent offshoots or developments of a deeper religious conviction or blueprint in the minds of people who thought very differently from the way we do in the modern world. This masked aspect can best be approached by questioning whether the Nasca Lines are indeed really lines.

Spirit paths?

The concept of the ground markings being 'lines' only really came into being after the 1930s, when people began observing them from aircraft. On the ground, the features can take on a different aspect. Researchers have found deeply worn foot tracks within the geometric outlines of some of the straight lines.[11] The Nasca 'lines' were walked, and repeatedly so by many feet, probably over considerable periods of time. Some align towards the ruins of Cahuachi off to one side of the Nasca *pampa*, a complex of former pyramids and temples that is believed to have been an oracle and pilgrimage centre.[12] Others seem to start nowhere in particular and end at no destination that we can today recognize as meaningful.

But the lines are constructed linear features containing the footpaths, so they are surely at least sacred routes and not merely mundane trails, and in that sense they are geoglyphs. As American archeologist Jay von Werlhof has said of

The water association, if valid, seems to be more with the flow of water across the *pampa*. Lines intersect now-dry riverbeds (*quebradas*) where they change direction, and the 'ray centres' are apparently situated where water issued out onto the *pampa*. The trapezoids are generally placed on elevated strips of land between the now-dry water courses, and their axes usually run parallel with what would have been the direction of water flow. A further possible water connection is with straight, subterranean aqueducts around the valley edges of the *pampa*, though there is a debate as to whether these are as old as the Nasca Lines or were introduced by the ancient linear features in the United States: 'While geoglyphs and trails did have separate particular roles, generically they fulfilled similar spiritual purposes.'[13] He notes that the Mojave people of the south-western United States treat both geoglyphs and sacred trails as having been made by the same spirit creators. This apparent obsessive walking of the lines gives us a clue that most Nasca researchers have failed to note; it is a clue that lies far to the north of Nasca in the territory of the Kogi people of northern Colombia.

Kogi Indians walk ancient stone paths as a religious observance, as a devotional exercise like the telling of rosary beads. The Kogi *mamas* or shamans say that they also travel the paths in their trances, because they are the physical traces of paths in the spirit otherworld, which they call *aluna*. With their dreamy shamanic vision, the *mamas* can see spirit paths continuing straight on beyond the point where the physical paths end. The ritualized sweeping of the physical roads is seen as a religious act as well – as seems to have been the case with some of the Nasca Lines.

So in a living South American Indian tradition, we are told that the old paths are physical traces of otherworld routes, and this may be the common underlying motif concerning obsessively straight ancient ways throughout the Americas. The exact straightness gave them a sense of otherness, of not quite being in this world, of being an interface with the invisible spirit realms. It imbued them with an aura of supernatural power that was appropriated by priests and rulers in various cultures to augment their claims to authority. The spiritual power symbolized by such linear features could be used to sanctify religious, ceremonial and military processions and movement. And yet even this may be only the tip of an iceberg. The Kogi are a remnant of the earlier Taironas culture, and it was they

who constructed the sacred paths. Their culture seemingly blossomed when they introduced the use of mind-altering mushrooms to their religious system. This raises another, closely related issue, which is typically overlooked.

Hallucinogens and entoptic phenomena

Whether it runs contrary to our current cultural views or not, the fact is that a great many pre-Columbian native peoples took mind-altering drugs as part of their religious activities.[14] In Mexico, the Olmec licked hallucinogenic toads, among other mind-altering substances; the Maya and the

BELOW Ayahuasca is a powerful hallucinogen that has been used by Amazonian Indians for generations. It is made using the *Banisteriopsis caapi* vine.

Aztecs took a whole pharmacopoeia of hallucinogens contained in certain seeds, beans, plants and mushrooms; Native Americans of northern Mexico and the southern United States favoured the mescaline-containing peyote cactus and various forms of datura, such as jimson weed. To this day, powerful hallucinogens like ayahuasca (infusions made from the *Banisteriopsis caapi* vine mixed with certain other plants) or snuffs made from psychoactive plants are taken by Amazonian Indians, as they have been for untold generations.

The people of the Andes were no different. Enormous amounts of mind-altering drugs were consumed as sacraments along the whole cordillera. The northern Peruvian oracle temple and pilgrimage location of Chavin de Huantar (*c.* 2000–900 BCE), for example, was at the centre of a widespread cult involving the ingestion of hallucinogens, as has already been mentioned (see page 68). The mescaline-containing San Pedro cactus is carved on a stone panel there, depicted as being held by a masked shaman or priest, like a staff of office. Even Chavin-culture

artwork was what we might call psychedelic, using visual ambiguities and the play of sunlight and shadow to create shifting or morphing effects.[15] Again, further south, archeologists investigating the ruins of the huge Tiahuanaco ceremonial and pilgrimage centre in Bolivia uncovered snuff trays, inhalation tubes and other equipment recognized as being widely used in ancient and some modern tribal societies in South America for the consumption of hallucinogenic substances. Depictions of the San Pedro cactus were also found, like the one at Chavin. Also like Chavin, Tiahuanaco was the centre of a religious cult that extended widely through the Andes, and this existed contemporaneously with the creation of the Nasca (and doubtless other Andean) lines.

The presence of traditions using such widely consumed mind-altering drugs may well account for that often-noted characteristic of the Nasca and other geoglyphs – they are most clearly seen from the air. It has been argued that this was because they were laid out for the benefit of flying gods, such as Kon Virachocha, but in 1977 anthropologist Marlene Dobkin de Rios put forward a more specific suggestion. She concluded that the lines were terrestrial depictions of entoptic phenomena,[16] an interpretation that I came to, independently, some years later.[17] Entoptic phenomena are geometric patterns that are produced in the visual cortex of the eye during trance states, especially drug-induced trance states, as well as during certain neurological conditions.[18] This neurological imagery is used by some drug-taking Amazonian tribes to this day as a basis for their tribal artwork. Many of the Andean societies involved in the production and use of linear features were either shamanic or had developed from shamanic origins – shamanism was an early religious and healing practice that had some form of ecstatic trance experience at its core, interpreted as the aerial journey of the shaman's spirit – the sort of sensation we might refer to today as an out-of-body experience, or, in more medical terminology, as a dissociative mental state.

The flight of the soul

This core experience of the flight of the soul is represented worldwide in shamanic iconography in the form of bird-related symbolism. The cultural circumstances and details of expression of shamanism may vary, but the basic, neurologically driven out-of-body sensation is cross-cultural: it is universal in entranced states, whether created by drugs, trauma or another cause.

Put in its simplest terms, Dobkin de Rios's suggestion is that the straight landscape line motif originated in the entoptic imagery produced by the ecstatic experience at the heart of shamanism – it could be said that the lines are an archaic graphic version of the 'tunnel' often reported in today's near-death experiences, along which the nearly dying person seems to float towards a bright light. It is directly linked to the sensation of the spirit moving out of the

body. Therefore straightness may have been, by association, linked to the idea of flight – 'as the crow flies', we say. And that might underlie the 'airline directness' of so many of these linear features. Dobkin de Rios also cited Peruvian pottery decorated with images of flying figures, some of them holding what appear to be mushrooms.

What all Nasca researchers agree on is that Erich Von Daniken's 'Chariots of the Gods' notion that the Nasca Lines were runways for extraterrestrial craft is nonsense. Anyone who has examined the structural nature of the lines can see that they could never have been runways of any sort, quite apart from other evidential factors that destroy the fantasy, which is a crude modern projection onto ancient sacred geography and an insult to the complexity of pre-Columbian thought. The lines at Nasca are a legacy left by the ancient American Indian mind and soul, not by ancient astronauts. That alone holds the secret of the straightness.

LEFT **Detail of a prehistoric rock painting in the White Shaman Shelter near Seminole Canyon, Texas. The "white shaman" is shown rising out of a similar dark shape. This 4,000-year-old painting is thought to depict the shaman undergoing an out-of-body experience while in trance.**

Flying to the otherworld

Other sites provide evidence of associations between altered states of consciousness and straight lines in the Americas, and we can look at three examples here. One recently examined on the ground by the present author had been found as a result of information gleaned from ethnological archives.

RIGHT **At Sears Point, a semi-circle of rocks, seen here in the foreground, forms a vision quest site where an entranced shaman would have sat to look down the ground line toward the rock at the other end. The line is now darkened with age, but it can just be made out.**

Papago Foot

The ethnological account dates to the end of the 19th century, and was given by Papago Foot, a shaman of the Gila River area in Arizona. He stated that when he was a young man he went to a sacred cave in a butte (a flat-topped hill with steep sides) near Tempe, in modern-day Phoenix, Arizona, and smoked a special 'reed' cigarette that put him into a trance in which he had a powerful vision. A spirit appeared to him in human form, saying that he would help Papago Foot become a shaman. 'The spirit tied a cobweb from that butte to Tempe Butte, and thence to Four Peaks, to the San Francisco Mountains ... and thence to Avikwame at Needles. He travelled on that

cobweb and had various cures revealed to him at each butte.'[19] ('Avikwame' is Avikwa'ame, Spirit Mountain, which harbours the rock-art-emblazoned Grapevine Canyon, mentioned earlier, see page 67.)

Anthropologist Leslie Spier further confirmed that the Indians 'think of the buttes as connected by strings... The dreamer thinks he is moved along the string through the air...' Such invisible 'strings' and 'cobwebs' stretched tautly through the air were surely the spectral version of lines marked on the ground, in the way that the Kusan Sum of the Maya are the invisible version of the physical *sacbeob* or straight causeways (see page 73).

Papago Foot's out-of-body spirit journey along these strings or web filaments fits neatly into the general idea of the lines being otherworld routes. The cave that Papago Foot mentions still exists, and the linear links between the peaks mentioned can be mapped, forming a virtual sacred geography hovering in the air, interacting with the physical topography.

Sears Point

Another example is at Sears Point in the Gila River valley in southern Arizona. There are about 50 ground drawings here, and one of them, on a low mesa or flat tableland, takes the form of a straight line scored on the ground, and is so old that the once-yellow line shining out bright against the dark pebbles of the desert pavement has now become darkened itself, so that it is a subtle

feature. At the eastern end of the line is a rock with a notch in its upper edge; at the other, western end of the line is a semicircle of rocks, the sort of feature that often marks a vision-quest site or 'bed' – remote locations where individuals went to seek a vision by means of fasting, sleep deprivation and sometimes other mind-altering practices such as the taking of hallucinogens.

Sitting within this arc of stones and looking down the line, the peak of a mountain sacred to the Yuman and Pima people is visible through the notch in the rock. At the summer solstice in June, the sun can be seen to rise out of the peak when viewed along the ground line.[20] In the way that old Papago Foot travelled to the sacred mountains by means of a cobweb, so Yuman shamans flew to the sacred peaks in out-of-body trance visions. We can be sure that the sun rising or setting over the peaks at the solstices or equinoxes would represent especially auspicious moments, and that the straight line on the Sears Point mesa was the 'trajectory' guideline along which the shaman's spirit travelled in trance to the mountains. We know that native shamans in the region used jimson-weed infusions to go into their trance 'dreams', in which, they said, they saw the rocks and pebbles on the ground shine in rainbow colours.

Hopewell earthworks

Then we have the gigantic, geometrically precise earthworks, ceremonial causeways and a relatively recently discovered dead-straight ceremonial road some 96 km (60 miles) long left by the Hopewell tribes in Ohio and adjacent states. The earthworks included mounds, truncated earthen pyramids (probably temple platforms) and circular, square or hexagonal earthen enclosures covering several hectares.

The Hopewell (c. 150 BCE–c. 500 CE) were a consortium of tribes subscribing to certain shamanic religious traditions. A copper-covered wooden effigy of a psychoactive mushroom was found in the grave of one shaman, who had been buried with his antler headgear. A great many Hopewell artefacts have been found expressing bird symbolism, classically associated with the trance 'flight' of the shaman.

Overall, it would seem to be the case that the straight-line mystery in the ancient Americas cannot be properly addressed unless archeologists – unhampered by their own culture's attitude to psychoactive drugs – understand the major role that altered states of consciousness played in the pre-Columbian world. The drug-taking is fundamental to decoding many of the sacred geographies of the American native.

Otherworld routes of the Stone Age

It is not only in the Americas that enigmatic, prehistoric linear land features are to be found. Scattered at locations all around the British Isles are several dozen giant earthen monuments called 'cursuses'. These are parallel-sided features defined by low earthen banks and shallow ditches or the socket holes of what had been timber posts.

Cursus size and naming

Ranging in length from short features right up to 10 km (6 miles), cursuses and have geometrically precise square or rounded ends – where these still survive. It would seem that the significance of a cursus to its builders was not in showy monumentalization, but rather in the demarcation of a sizeable linear strip of landscape. Consequently, most cursuses are discovered from aircraft by the identification of crop marks, because in the majority of cases their slight structures have virtually disappeared from view at ground level. 'Simply to state that cursuses are overwhelmingly straight monuments does them scant justice,' states one of their archeological investigators, Roy Loveday.[21] Looking at some of the larger ones from the air, he remarks that 'it appears as if a vast ruler had been used to score parallel lines across the landscape'. To get a real idea of scale, a larger cursus could contain more than

RIGHT **The Scorton cursus in Lancashire, England, seen here as dark, parallel crop markings running diagonally across the left-hand field. There are many theories for the existence of these closed-off linear strips but none of them is conclusive.**

LEFT **Bronze Age stonerows, Dartmoor National Park, England. These rows, like others on British moorlands and in Carnac, Brittany, typically link to prehistoric burial or cremation sites. The rows were perhaps spirit paths, and the large blocking stones at their ends, as seen here, intended to contain the spirits.**

20 football fields within its area, and one that ran across the western end of what is now London's Heathrow airport dwarfed the runways that now accommodate jumbo jets there.

The curious name 'cursus' (Latin for racecourse) was given to the monument type by the observant 18th-century antiquarian William Stukeley, who recognized subtle linear earthworks extending for nearly 3 km (2 miles) close to Stonehenge as a monumental feature, one that he interpreted as being a Romano-British racecourse. Although cursuses are now known to be much more ancient features 4,000 or more years old, belonging to the Neolithic (later Stone Age) era of prehistory, the name stuck.

Cursus significance

Nobody has much of a clue as to what the purpose of cursuses might have been. Excavations have revealed very little – cursuses have rightly been described as 'vast empty enclosures'. They were not for burial of the dead, and they were not mortuary enclosures, as had originally been supposed. Various explanatory suggestions have since been put forward – astronomical alignment, although these do not work at all for most cursuses, processional routes, symbolic rivers, and so forth – but none are convincing.

By cross-referencing with features in the Americas such as the Andean lines and Mayan causeways, we may have in cursuses another version, half the world away, of otherworld routes. Perhaps they were for the navigation of spirits rather than physical people. They typically connect burial sites: so were cursuses spirit ways, or perhaps compounds for containing spirits? If one follows this idea, new perspectives come into view. The purpose of the cursus endpoints could be interpreted as to block the spirits of the ancestors from wandering abroad into the living human world.

There are hints of this as well with the blocking stones at the ends of prehistoric stone rows on English moorlands and in Brittany. These linear features also relate in some way to places of the dead, and on Dartmoor (as at Carnac in Brittany) the stone rows could run for considerable lengths and often in parallel rows. The terminal stones were often larger than those in the rows, and set at right angles to the row as if to block something. Block what? Surely the movement of the spirits of those interred in the sites with which the lines of stones connect?

The geography of death

*A medieval feature in Britain and continental Europe might just possibly have evoked an extremely archaic, deep-rooted spirit belief that informed the cursus and stone-row monuments. The feature is a special class of old pathway – the 'corpse road'. In Britain it was also known by various other names, including church path or churchway, lyke or lych way (from the Old English **liches**, or corpse) or burial road, to name just some. Many have disappeared, while the original purposes of those that survive as footpaths have been largely forgotten.*

Corpse roads as flight paths

Basically they functioned as specialized routes to enable isolated communities to carry their dead to the churches that held the parish burial rights. But they had a secret history, too. The corpse roads not only crossed the physical countryside, but also ran through the mindscapes of pre-industrial country folk, and a spirit lore became attached to them. This is revealed by a variety of related 'virtual' and physical features to be found across Old Europe.

The virtual features were folk beliefs that had a geographical reality. An example

existed in Nemen (formerly in Germany, now in Russia), where there was the tradition of a *Leichenflugbahn*, literally 'corpse flight path'. There were two cemeteries in the town, and spirits were believed to travel between the two places along a direct course close to the ground, so a straight line connecting the two places was kept clear of fences, walls and buildings so that they would not be obstructed. The Germans also had similar virtual paths, they called *Geisterwege* that linked actual, physically real cemeteries. Although conceptual, these spirit paths had a definite geography in local folklore, and people would be sure to avoid them at night. A German folklore handbook tells us that they ran 'in a straight line over mountains and valleys and through marshes... In towns they pass the houses closely or go right through them.'[22]

Spirit lore

In Ireland and other Celtic countries there were straight fairy paths that, although invisible, had such perceived geographical reality in people's minds that building practices were adopted to ensure their unobstructed passage. Fairies and the spirits of the dead held a curiously ambiguous relationship in the peasant mind.[23]

The actual, physical corpse roads of Britain and continental Europe vary between being dead-straight and not particularly straight. Notably straight ones include medieval Dutch *Doodwegen* (death roads) and *Spokenwegen* (spook or ghost roads), which were officially checked on an annual basis to ensure they remained straight and had a regular width. These appear to be rather more exact versions of British corpse roads.

The archaic spirit lore that was attached to the corpse ways and the 'virtual' ways for the spirits of the dead was alluded to in Shakespeare's *A Midsummer Night's Dream*, where that old land spirit, Puck, says:

Now it is the time of night,
That the graves, all gaping wide,
Every one lets forth his sprite,
In the church-way paths to glide.[24]

Banishing the spirits

There were all sorts of ritualistic ruses resorted to by those transporting the corpse to ensure that its spirit did not return and haunt the living – or even wander as an animated corpse, for the belief in revenants was widespread in medieval Europe.[25] It was further believed that church paths leading to and from cemeteries needed to be swept at certain times of year so as to dislodge the spirits haunting them. Occasionally 'spirit traps' (webs of thread on a framework) were placed on them to snare flitting phantoms.

Across Europe there were variations on a whole connected divinatory system that involved necromantic activities in churchyards, at crossroads, stiles, prehistoric burial mounds – and corpse or death roads. In Holland such diviners were known as 'precursors'.[26]

It is surely clear that from prehistory up to late medieval and even early modern times, in various parts of the world, sacred geographies involving straight landscape lines were almost certainly connected with the mapping of what was perceived as spirit movement through physical topographies, whether the spirits of the dead, of entranced, out-of-body shamans or nature spirits. Straight landscape lines were involved with the cartography of the otherworld.

ABOVE According to folklore, this granite stile on a corpse road leading to Ludgvan church, Cornwall, was used for necromantic divination in centuries past.

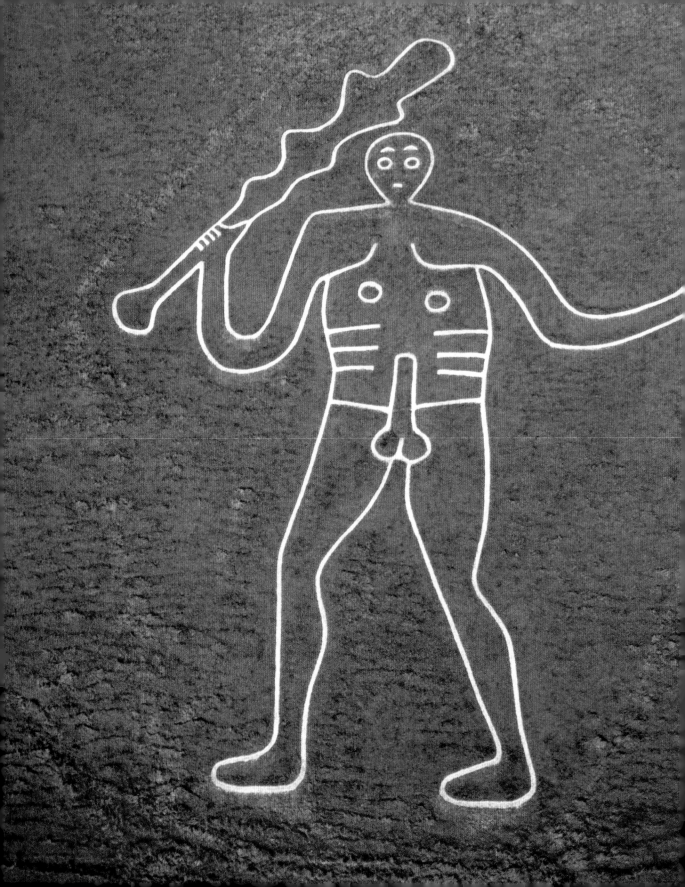

GIANTS IN THE EARTH
Ground Patterns, Images and Effigies

*S*traight lines and ritual roads were not the only markings emblazoned directly onto the land – there were also abstract patterns, meandering lines, geometric and figurative images and effigies. These images and linear features often shared the same landscapes, so presumably had related origins, even if not the same meanings. Generally, these landscapes were those occupied by shamanic peoples, so we use the term 'shamanic landscapes' to label them.

The geoglyphs were marked in various ways on the ground, dependent on the local circumstances: by scouring into the ground, usually on desert surfaces, and often referred to as 'intaglios'; by laying out the imagery with small rocks and boulders and technically referred to as 'petroforms' or 'boulder mosaics'; or they were created by means of engineered earthworks. As with the straight linear features, most of these geoglyphs and effigy mounds now survive best in the Americas.

Ground drawings and patterns

The Nasca Lines of Peru (see page 72) appear to be superimposed on an arguably earlier landscape containing ground drawings of figurative forms such as birds, monkeys, spiders, lizards, whales and flowers, as well as geometric forms like spirals and irregular, abstract shapes. These geoglyphs range from about 15 metres (50 feet) to more than 305 metres (1,000 feet) in length.

ABOVE Figurative ground drawings at Nasca are each formed by a single, unbroken line. This has led to speculation that they were for processional use.

They are unicursal in nature, meaning that each one is formed by a single line that traces an unbroken course that does not cross over itself. This factor has raised speculation that they were for dance or processional use. On the slopes of a *pampa* plateau in the Nasca area there is also a huge, if somewhat crude, image of a human being with its right arm raised as if in greeting or salute.

Other Andean geoglyphs

A ten-year (1997–2007) research effort in the Palpa region 40 km (25 miles) north of Nasca, by German researchers using a range of multi-disciplinary techniques including excavation, global-positioning data and photogrammetric mapping, has resulted in the discovery on *pampa* plateaus and valley sides of not only linear features, but several hundred hitherto unnoticed figurative geoglyphs, including images representing both human and animal figures, as well as something that looks like a knife plus geometric designs. They also uncovered small stone buildings in which offerings were found, seemingly related to water and fertility rituals, and rectangular temples or tombs with labyrinthine interior walls that appear to be dedicated to the dead – presumably indicating ancestor worship or perhaps an oracular cult. The researchers, who recognize the ground markings as comprising ritual landscapes, think that these Palpa geoglyphs pre-date those in the Nasca area. The full results of this major research programme are only beginning to be published at the time of writing.[1]

On the sandy seaward slopes of the Bay of Paracas, approximately 97 km (60 miles) north of Ica, there is an almost 183-metre (600-foot)-long intaglio of a three-pronged design. Known variously as the 'Candelabra of the Andes' and the 'Trident of Paracas', this ground marking is almost inaccessible on the ground, but can be seen many miles out to sea. It has been dated to 200 BCE, but could be older. One researcher, Frank Joseph, has noticed that it looks very similar to a rock carving in Cleveland Natural Park,

California, which is thought to be a stylized representation of the hallucinogenic jimson weed (*Datura stramonium*). He speculates that the ancient Paracas people may have voyaged up the west coast of the Americas to obtain the weed.[2]

About 967 km (600 miles) southwards along the Andean cordillera from the Nasca–Palpa region are approximately 5,000 intaglios of llamas, lizards, birds, fish, crosses, geometric patterns and some human-like forms inscribed on the Atacama Desert of northern Chile. Most of them fall along ancient llama caravan routes that ran east–west between the Andes and the Pacific coast, and north–south between desert oases – some geoglyph groups even depict long lines of llamas and alpacas.

The sizes of the geoglyphs range to more than 115 metres (370 feet) in height, the tallest being the so-called 'Atacama Giant', a masked shaman or chieftain. The technique in the main is not etching into the ground as at Nasca and Palpa, but the creation of light areas to form the images by the clearance of dark pebbles that are scattered over the desert surface. There is some evidence that the geoglyphs may date to *c*. 500 BCE, but as yet little appears to be known about them for certain.

Patterns in the Californian wilderness

A similar type of environment is to be found in Death Valley, California. This is so remote and arid that it is easy to understand why few people would ever guess of the ancient sacred cartography of ritual pathways, shrines, vision-quest beds and curious sinuous lines and weird patterns of rocks that it harbours. The valley is 153 km (95 miles) long and 40 km (25 miles) wide, adjacent to the Nevada state line. People inhabited Death Valley from about 9,000 years ago, when a cool period caused a shallow lake to occupy the valley floor. Eventually warmer, arid conditions developed, and it had dried up by about 2,000 years ago. Whereas the region looks inhospitable to modern eyes, the collective territory of the valley, the adjacent Panamint Valley and the nearby Coso

LEFT A figurative geoglyph on the slope of a small hill in the Palpa region has been interpreted in modern times as an astronaut or spaceman but more likely represents a shaman or Nazca priest, someone with magic powers who could predict the weather.

BELOW In the Bay of Paracas in Peru there is a 183-metre (600-foot)-long intaglio known as the Trident of Paracas. It may be a representation of the hallucinogenic jimson weed.

ABOVE **The Atacama Giant is a masked shaman formed by the clearance of pebbles to expose light areas of the desert surface. It lies among a collection of about 5000 intaglios thought to date from as early as 500 BCE**

Mountains to the west, and the wilderness stretching to Charleston Peak outside Las Vegas to the east, was known to the Shoshone as *tiwiniyarivipi* – 'where the stories begin and end' or 'mythic land, sacred country'.[3] The Death Valley geoglyphs are to be found in remote locations across that magic land and take various forms. They are extremely fragile and sensitive to damage, and so their precise locations are kept fairly secret, but here we can look at just a few examples of what Death Valley has to offer.

One ground marking is situated on a low volcanic hillock near the salt flat known as the Devil's Golf Course. It has a cover of small volcanic rocks and pebbles, and cutting across it is a path made by the careful removal of this rock litter, much as is the case with the Atacama geoglyphs. Although the path crosses the whole hill, it comes from nowhere and goes to no destination in the surrounding terrain – it belongs just to the hill, and is a sacred path. Its course passes through or by the remains of various ritual features on the hill, including three stone mounds in a cleared area forming a shrine or sacred enclosure. Where the path enters and exits the cleared area, small arrangements of stone are laid out, interpreted by their early archeological investigator, Jay von Werlhof, as 'spirit

breaks' to protect the shrine area from any unwanted supernatural influences passing along the path. Also in the complex are vision-quest sites, and scatters of quartz, which was a vitally important magical stone to the native peoples.

Another kind of Death Valley geoglyph, a petroform, is to be found on a mesa-like fan (a flat-topped ridge) not far from Nevares Spring. The top of this fan is devoid of vegetation, and is covered by a dark veneer of pebbles lightly cemented in place by the effects of the harsh conditions. There is a complex of markings and features, but the most immediately obvious element is a long, meandering line of small rocks.

Intaglios are also to be found in the valley, such as a long, curving line scraped on a mesa top at Mustard Canyon. Alongside it is a small, intricate circular arrangement of stones that von Werlhof calls a 'ritualistic shaman's hearth'.[4] This was never used as an actual fireplace, but probably marked a shaman's vision-quest site.

RIGHT **A mysterious prehistoric line of rocks in Death Valley meanders across the landscape.**

Weather magic?

There are dozens of other geoglyphs of various kinds in the valley, and in the parallel Panamint Valley and in areas further west and south. They often comprise complexes of alignments, meanders, grids and irregular enclosures, and may extend for hundreds of metres. What could have been their purpose?

Von Werlhof thinks that, essentially, they were about weather magic. He suggests that the long-ago shamans of native groups living in the valley tried to put a brake on the encroaching aridity – it was part of a shaman's duties. It may seem strange to us that the laying out of ground markings should be seen as a magical act, but we know from the ethnology of the Yuman people in southern Arizona that their shamans, at least, did make marks on the ground as part of their deployment of supernatural power. In war, for example, the shaman might scratch a line in the ground between the contending parties. 'The line represented a mountain, the long Sierra Estrella,' the ethnologist Leslie Spier wrote. 'While the line that was drawn may have been a mark beyond which the enemy were dared to come, it was thought of as a mountain magically raised to give protection.'[5]

Precisely the same form of magic was used to thwart opponents in intertribal races: one runner would run ahead of another and draw a line across his path to symbolize (or, in some magical way, act as if it actually was) a deep canyon or a mountain that prevented his opponent from continuing. In one recorded instance, a Maricopa shaman drew a line across the course of a race between runners of the Maricopa and Pima tribes. 'The Maricopa racer got by, but when the Pima came up, he stood stock still: he did not know what to do.'[6] A Pima shaman had to lead him around the 'mountain' – the line – so that he could race on.

The research of a current archeological investigator of the region, David Whitley, suggests an alternative interpretation of some of the Panamint and Death Valley geoglyphs. He notes that vision questing could involve not only days of fasting, going without sleep and praying, but also 'ritual exertion' such as running or the handling of heavy rocks – as would be involved in the laying out of the stone lines and patterns.[7] If this explanation is correct, then some geoglyphs in and around Death Valley were a consequence of lonely vision quests conducted by the ancient shamans.

BELOW The Devil's Golf Course in Death Valley features a path made by the removal of rock litter. It has no logical beginning or end but vision quest sites, quartz and an enclosure with shrines all point to it being a sacred path.

The giants of the Colorado River Valley

South from Death Valley, intaglio figures that seem to have had a different function are to be found in the Colorado River Valley, which forms the boundary between Arizona and southern California. Probably the most famous of these figures is the 'Giant', on a terrace above the river near Blythe on the California side of the river.

ABOVE **The Blythe Giant of the Colorado River Valley could be a representation of the culture-hero Mastamho.**

This intaglio is about 18 metres (60 feet) long and is part of a complex of geoglyphs, which include two other large human figures, a four-legged animal of some indeterminate kind, a concentric circle and a spiral. Another giant figure is on the desert near Winterhaven. On the Arizona side of the river there is an intaglio of a rattlesnake with twin rocks placed for its eyes (near the township of Parker) and, in a remote and semi-secret location, another depicting a running figure above a wavy line representing water, below which are representations of fish. The figure is holding a spear, its shaft a geoglyph, its

point made up of small pieces of white quartz. It looks as if the figure is about to spear a fish.

The lines of this large geoglyph have oxidized and darkened over the centuries, and although it is now difficult to see at close quarters, it is a key image because it is thought the figure represents the god and culture-hero Mastamho, who created the Colorado River and the whole world. It could be that he is also represented by the Blythe Giant on the other side of the river. Indeed, it is generally considered that many of the human and animal figures inscribed on the desert terraces along the valley relate to mythological characters and events of the Yuman people.

Pilgrimage stations

The intaglios are thought to have been made over many centuries; scientific attempts at dating desert varnish (dust that builds up, forming a dark patina) on them indicate that the earliest ones may range from *c.* 1000 BCE to *c.* 900 CE. Fragmentary ethnological evidence indicates that at least some of the intaglios were stations on a Yuman pilgrimage route that ran from Pilot Knob at the southern end of the river (mythically the spirit house where the dead dwell) to the previously mentioned Avikwa'ame or Spirit Mountain further north (see page 67), built by Mastamho and from where he created the world.

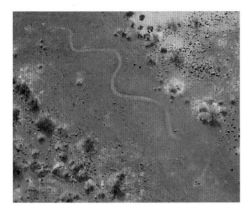

'At the various ceremonial stops along this route, an officiating shaman would instruct the participants in mythic history and ritually re-enact mythic events,' informs David Whitley.[8]

The pilgrimage route retraced the path of Masthamo in his mythic travels and activities, very much in the manner that an Australian Aboriginal dream-journey route or 'songline' retraces the route of a Dreamtime being. Spirit Mountain was noted far and wide as being a place of great supernatural power, and for possibly thousands of years was visited by shamans, who in a trance re-experienced the mythic events of the creation, and in vision met the mythic beings involved. As noted already (see page 67), the mountain is a major rock-art site, containing hundreds of engravings.

Vision-quest activities

Near the northern end of the Colorado River Valley is an obscure, self-contained inscribed landscape that was probably not directly connected with the pilgrimage parade of geoglyphs. It is composed of straight lines laid out in an organized, cross-hatched pattern. The lines are actually furrows in the desert ground, and were apparently tracks along which Native American braves ran intensively, probably as part of vision-quest activities.

Such arduous running was (and still is) quite widely practised by some native tribes as a way of speeding the onset of exhaustion to facilitate the sought-after visionary state of consciousness, or, in fact, to act as the vision-quest activity in itself. There are accounts of such sacred running in the ethnological records. For instance, Papago tribespeople would make a week-long pilgrimage from Arizona to the ocean, and then certain of the pilgrims would engage in intensive running for 32 km (20 miles) towards a headland and the same distance back again in order to enter a dream-like state. One runner saw a mountain slowly revolve in front of him as he ran, while another heard a voice saying that the Ocean Shaman wanted to see him, causing him to retire to a cave for four years where he learned sacred songs. Sometimes the extreme exertion involved in such sacred running proved fatal.[9]

LEFT **One of the Colorado River Valley intaglios depicts a rattlesnake with rocks placed for its eyes. Intaglios such as these helped to tell a story of the Yuman people.**

LEFT **The running figure is thought to be the god Mastamho who created the Colorado River. Shamans would ritually re-enact mythic events at intaglios such as these, which formed stations aong a pilgrimage route.**

Petroform landscapes and effigy mounds

*Geoglyphs of another kind survive in the Canadian province of Manitoba,
where a number of boulder-mosaic or petroform sacred landscapes are to be
found at various locations in the forested wilderness of Whiteshell Provincial
Park. They are the largest such landscapes in North America. The two main
focal areas are Tie Creek and Bannock Point.*

The seat of the Great Spirit

Of these two, Tie Creek is the one that is
best preserved, because it is the remotest
and access is only allowed with a guide
approved by the local Anishinabe (Ojibway)
people. The petroform locations are broad
areas of table-rock scraped clear by glaciers
tens of thousands of years ago, on which
abstract and figurative designs, both large
and small, have been laid out by an
unknown people long ago using small rocks.
The designs include large-scale abstract and
geometric patterns, such as lines, grids,
curved and radial settings, as well as smaller
depictions of snakes and even wolf and bear
paw marks 1 metre (3 feet) or so across

made from rocks, as if giant versions of these creatures had padded in from the surrounding forest. There are also a few lightly marked sinuous lines that wander, seemingly aimlessly, over the table-rock areas between the main design features.

At the approach to the Tie Creek petroform landscape is a natural boulder resembling a buffalo at rest (see page 27), which would in itself have signified the sanctity of the area – indeed, an area so sacred that it is known as Manito Ahbee, 'Where the Great Spirit Sits', and gives its name to the entire province of Manitoba.

At Bannock Point there are numerous small turtle-shaped rings of rocks that seem to have been vision-quest 'beds'. Ritual activity and religious observance are still undertaken at these petroform sites, and votive cloths tied to trees and the timber frames of longhouses and sweat lodges are to be found close to the petroform designs.

The considerable antiquity of some of the features is indicated by dense lichen growth around the rocks, but their exact age is uncertain. Archeologists have dated the remnants of a campsite found among the ground markings to *c.* 500 CE. Present-day Anishinabe lore states that the designs were laid out by the First People.

There are various claims about the meaning of the petroforms in current First Nation, native lore, especially the idea that

they are large-scale versions of the bark scrolls traditionally used by Anishinabe people for teaching purposes. Others may have been depictions of sweat lodges, and culture heroes, particularly Waynaboozhoo, the First Anishinabe. But today's tribespeople do not claim that their interpretations of the ground patterns are necessarily the only, or correct, ones.

Earthen enigmas

The greatest known concentration of effigy mounds in the world is in the Upper Midwest of the United States. The focal area is Wisconsin, but the mounds extend into parts of Iowa, Illinois and Minnesota. In Wisconsin alone it is estimated that there were originally more than 100 main groups of effigy mounds, comprising some 15,000 individual features.

ABOVE **At Bannock Point, where Indian rituals still sometimes take place, there are several turtle-shaped rings of rock, many of them ancient, that mark vision quest places.**

LEFT **One of the petroform designs at Tie Creek depicts a giant bear paw print, as if a huge creature had walked the land in that very spot.**

Although most effigy mounds are now lost, having been ploughed out or built over, some still survive and can be well seen in preserved areas like Effigy Mounds National Monument on the Iowa bank of the Mississippi. The mounds depict a variety of animals, including birds, bears, wolves, long-tailed creatures called 'panthers' and 'lizards', turtles and deer, together with some hybrid human-bird forms and nine complete human figures. There are also a greater number of mounds with geometric ground plans that have been categorized as linear, oval, conical and biconical. In south-western Wisconsin there are 'chain' or compound mound groups consisting of long strings of conical mounds connected by linear embankments.

Late Woodland culture

Effigy mounds were built between *c.* 700 and 1200 CE by what archeologists call the Late Woodland culture. These people continued and developed earlier mound-building traditions. 'Sometime after AD 700, the construction of mounds greatly accelerated, and Late Woodland people ... began a spectacular custom that involved sculpting hilltops and other prominent locations into sometimes huge ceremonial complexes that consisted of effigy mounds,' inform the Wisconsin effigy-mound experts, Robert Birmingham and Leslie Eisenberg.[10] Round or rectangular earthen enclosures accompanied some mound groups.

A mound seems to have been built in a single effort. Some mounds were built over intaglio versions of an effigy dug up to a metre (3 feet) into the ground. Evidence suggests that an intaglio was left open for some time, presumably for various ceremonial activities, and was then filled with ash, charcoal and coloured soils in preparation for the actual construction of the mound. Most mounds tend to be less than 2 metres (6 feet) in height, but can be very large in area. The largest surviving bird image is in the grounds of the Mendota State Hospital near Madison, Wisconsin,

RIGHT **The Effigy Mounds National Monument on the Iowa bank of the Mississippi depicts a variety of animals. The Marching Bear Group consists of ten bears and several bird mounds.**

and has a wingspan of just under 214 metres (700 feet). As with many of the mounds, it is impossible to appreciate from ground level the overall shape of the bird effigy, with its beaked head turned to one side and its wings outstretched. Aerial photography has revealed the vestigial remains of a bird effigy elsewhere with a 402-metre (1,320-foot) wingspan. A preserved human effigy, Man Mound, near Baraboo, Wisconsin, is a little over 61 metres (200 feet), while a now-destroyed man mound near Lake Monona, Madison, was more than 214 metres (700 feet) long.

Most of the human effigies are shown with horns, which are thought to indicate buffalo-horn headdresses, commonly associated with shamans in Native American cultures of the region. Also, a shamanic culture-hero in local Winnebago (Ho-Chunk) myth, Red Horn, who undergoes a death–rebirth cycle, is believed to be depicted in 1,000-year-old pictograms in the remote Gottschall Rock Shelter in south-west Wisconsin. It could be that this is who is represented in the man mounds, for the creek that runs in front of the cave joins with the Wisconsin River 13 km (8 miles) away, where a cluster of man-bird and bird-effigy mounds existed: it has already been noted (see page 81) that bird symbolism is redolent of shamanism, and hybrid man-bird effigies specifically indicate shamanism. There is therefore little reason to doubt that these mounds, at least, had a shamanic connection.

Upper and Lower Worlds

In recent years a mix of detailed studies of motifs on Late Woodland pottery, tribal clan

ABOVE **Part of the Marching Bear Group viewed from the ground. Some mounds were built over intaglio versions of an effigy dug into the ground, then filled with ash, charcoal and coloured soils.**

structures, Winnebago myth and interpretations offered by living elders has started to give investigators glimpses into the meanings related to other earthen effigies. It appears that the creatures depicted in the shapes of the mounds fall into categories that express the Upper World (air) and Lower Worlds (earth and water) of Late Woodland cosmology.

Upper World creatures are birds and humans, and so the shamanic man-bird forms must also fall into this category. The bird effigies are often of the Thunderbird type, the deity whose eyes flash lightning and whose wings cause the thunder. These bird-related effigies are typically found among the hills of western Wisconsin, the portion of the state that lies underneath the 'Mississippi flyway' – the migration route of waterfowl and other birds.[11] Lower World earth-effigy creatures include bears, buffaloes, wolves, deer and elk. These are mainly found in western and central parts of Wisconsin. Lower World water creatures also include the long-tailed effigy forms.

For a long time these were identified as 'panthers' and 'lizards', but new studies now identify them as water spirits. Long-tailed water-spirit effigy mounds are concentrated in the low-lying eastern part of Wisconsin, which has an abundance of lakes, swamps and marshes. One group of long-tailed mounds, the so-called Lizard Mound Group near West Bend, Wisconsin, seemed to foil this distribution pattern, sitting as it does on a plateau well away

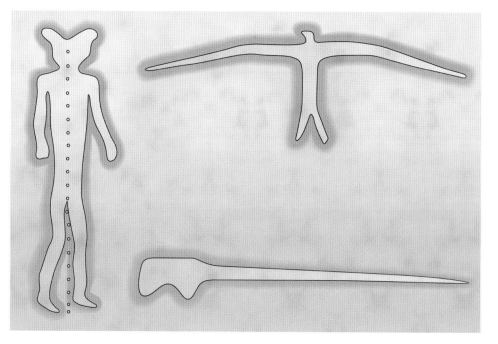

RIGHT **Effigy mounds take the form of long-tailed water spirits, birds and humans. Man Mound in Wisconsin is enormous - the dots down the centre of the figure are 3 metres (10 foot) apart.**

from major bodies of water, until it was realized that the site is located precisely on the headwaters of a branch of the Milwaukee River and is surrounded by numerous springs – places considered by virtually all ancient Native Americans as entrances to the spirit world.

Decoding the effigy enigma

The purpose of the effigy mounds remains unclear. Most of them contained burials, usually deposited in the head or heart region of the effigy. Also found in the mounds are arrangements of stones showing evidence of fire and burning, which are interpreted as altars. Small clay and rock receptacles of unknown purpose are commonly discovered inside the mounds too, and, like burials, usually occupy the heart or head areas of an effigy. These receptacles were sometimes placed inside a mound that does not contain a burial. In some cases, effigy mounds contain nothing at all – no burials, receptacles or altars. It is clear that the primary purpose of the mounds could not have been for burial, though death rituals were obviously often associated with them. And burial functions do not explain why the mounds had to be in the shapes of mythological beings; nor, as is the situation with virtually all geoglyphs, why they had to be on such a scale that they could not be appreciated at ground level, but only from some distance up in the air. There are three ways to answer this conundrum: the effigies did not have to be seen, but simply known to be in the form of the mound for symbolic purposes; the effigies were meant to be signs to the gods, not human beings; or the effigies were part of the spiritual geography of Late Woodland shamanism.

Whatever their deeper meaning, the mound complexes were presumably used for ceremonial purposes. 'The similarity of mound forms, mound arrangements, and

OTHER EFFIGY MOUNDS

Although the Upper Midwest has the greatest concentration of effigy mounds, they occur more sporadically elsewhere in the Americas. In Putnam County, Georgia, for example, there are stone effigy mounds, the best-known being the Rock Eagle mound. Made of quartz boulders and cobbles of other stone, the mound's wingspan is 36 metres (120 feet). It is also noteworthy that the great mound at the rather mysterious 3,000-year-old earthwork complex at Poverty Point, Louisiana, is thought to have originally been in the shape of a bird. And the Olmec centre of San Lorenzo, Mexico, was actually built on a man-made earthwork in the shape of a bird, possibly a condor, just over 1 km (¾ mile) long. So there seems to have been an extremely deep and long-lived propensity for the creation of such features in the ceremonial traditions of ancient American societies.

other customs attending mound construction found among the large effigy mound area argues for a shared sacred knowledge that may have been controlled by a society (perhaps secret) of religious specialists, such as shamans, who directed the mound-building ceremonials,' conclude Birmingham and Eisenberg.[12]

White on green

The urge to create landscape figures also existed outside ancient America, though probably in different social and ceremonial contexts. The best examples of such geoglyphs are the chalk hill figures of Britain. These were made by stripping away turf and shallow topsoil to reveal the underlying chalk, producing gleaming white images on the country's green and pleasant landscapes.

ABOVE Chalk hill figures in Britain were made by stripping away turf and soil to reveal white chalk beneath. The White Horse of Uffington in Oxfordshire is striking but its function is a mystery.

Many of the hill figures we can now see are relatively modern but there are a few that are certainly or probably ancient. One that possesses definite antiquity is the Uffington White Horse in Oxfordshire, 15 km (9 miles) east of Swindon.

The White Horse of Uffington
It is 110 metres (360 feet) in length and 40 metres (130 feet) tall, inscribed just below the brow of a hill that has the Iron Age earthworks of Uffington Castle on its summit. The location is within an area of even older prehistoric importance, with the Stone Age track known as the Ridgeway running close by, the Neolithic passage tomb of Wayland's Smithy almost 2 km (1 mile) away and the Blowing Stone, which issues sounds when blown into, nearby. The horse is a remarkable

graphic statement producing a strange but dynamic image of a horse with a rectangular head and beak-like mouth, a single undulating line depicting the creature's tail, back, neck and head, and four minimalist lines expressing its outstretched, galloping legs. Its single eye is a dome of chalk more than 1 metre (3 feet) in diameter. (Folklore states that a wish will come true if the person stands on the eye, turning while making the wish. Given the angle of the slope, this is not as easy as it sounds.)

At close quarters the horse is hard to see, and is best made out at a distance of 6–10 km (4–6 miles) to the north, or from the air. The reason for the poor close-up visibility is because the figure is now on the shoulder of the hill, and this is largely because it has crept up the hillside over many centuries due to recutting. Without recutting, the figure would have grown back into the ground and become invisible. In recent centuries (at least) there was the local Uffington festive event of 'scouring the horse' every seven years, at Whitsun or Michaelmas.

There was debate concerning the age of the horse for a great many years, with suggestions such as the one that the figure celebrated King Alfred's defeat of the Danes, or that it was a Saxon or Celtic tribal territorial image. The matter was settled after archeological investigation in 1996, when a new technique called 'Optical Stimulated Luminescence' was used – this can measure when soil was last exposed to sunlight. The investigators unearthed soil at the site that had not been disturbed and arrived at a set of dates ranging between *c.* 1400 and *c.* 900 BCE, covering the late Bronze Age to early Iron Age eras. The White Horse of Uffington was older than anyone had supposed. In the process of the dating excavations, the archeologists confirmed that the horse had crept uphill a short

distance, so would once have been more visible from the ground at closer quarters, and also found that its beak-like mouth had once been longer. Though the approximate age of the horse geoglyph is now known, its function remains a mystery.

The Long Man of Wilmington

Another probably ancient hill figure is the Long Man of Wilmington, in East Sussex, 15 km (9 miles) south-east of Lewes. It is on a curiously smooth, sloping side of Windover Hill and displays the outline of a human figure with bent arms, holding an upright stave or possibly a spear in each hand. The staves match the tallness of the figure, and are more than 70 metres (230 feet) in length. The geoglyph, now outlined with white concrete blocks, is elongated to compensate for the foreshortening effect of looking up the hill slope, though its proportions appear most correct only from the air.

It is known from documentary records that the figure was once called the Green Man because it had grown back into the hillside, though still discernible, and it has been subjected to recuttings in recent centuries, some of them rather brutal. There is a suspicion that the figure once

ABOVE **The Long Man of Wilmington in East Sussex lies on a hill directly below a Neolithic burial mound and is believed by some to depict a prehistoric priest or shaman.**

appeared a little different from what now survives: 18th-century drawings show facial features and other details and differently positioned feet, while a verbal description by James Levett in 1873 claimed that there was the image of a cock near the figure, although, if so, this has never been uncovered. In restorations in 1874 and 1969, fragments of what could have been Roman brickwork were found, thus suggesting that the geoglyph is at least as old as Roman times. Resistivity surveys of the ground around the Long Man revealed faint traces of what might have been a plume or other feature curving out of the top of the head, and what might have been a scythe at the top of one of the staves and a rake at the top of the other (in keeping with a drawing made in 1776), although the archeologists conducting the survey were at pains to point out that these findings were all extremely tentative.

The question of who the figure represents has brought forward a deluge of speculations over the centuries, including suggestions that the Long Man is, variously, a Celtic or Roman god, a mythic giant, a pilgrim, the Norse shaman-god Odin, Beowulf, Apollo, or even that he represents the Hindu deity Varuna. Plus many more besides. Put simply, nobody knows the identity of this enigmatic figure. But there is a strong school of thought that considers him to be a prehistoric priest or shaman figure, because on the crest of Windover Hill, above the Long Man's head, there is a Neolithic barrow (burial mound), of unusual length at 55 metres (180 feet). There are also traces of a cursus nearby.

Other hill figures

Another controversial hill figure is the Cerne Abbas Giant in Dorset, also engraved on a hillside. He is otherwise known as the Rude Man or Rude Giant. At 55 metres (180 foot) long and 51 metres (167 foot)

wide, he is formed by a trench measuring approximately 30 cm (12 inches) in width and depth. The figure wields a club and displays a 9-metre (30-foot) erect phallus.

Recent findings of archeological investigation have suggested that part of the carving has been lost and that the figure was originally depicted with a cloak over his left arm.

Opinion seems equally split as to whether the geoglyph's origins lie in Iron Age or Roman times, or is a mischievous 18th-century folly. There is no conclusive evidence to support any view but the figure is an important part of local culture and is often linked to fertility in local folklore.

Other hill figures exist in Britain with more tenuous claims to antiquity, while still others are definitely modern. One particularly interesting case is not a chalk figure, but one cut in a hillside rich in red oxide – the Red Horse of Tysoe, in Warwickshire. Modern filtered photographs of vegetation discolorations on the hillside indicate that there was an original horse figure approximately 91 metres (300 feet) long and 64 metres (210 feet) high. Though it is now long gone, its fame lasted over subsequent centuries, and further red horses of various sizes and shapes were cut in the hillside – a fact that has confused matters ever since. But further aerial survey, soil resistivity studies and crop-mark analysis have confirmed that there was indeed an early figure.[13] Traces of all of them have now effectively disappeared.

The age of, and reason for, the original horse are not known, but there are clues. The name Tysoe signifies 'spur of land dedicated to Tiw', a Germanic form of the Roman god Mars, who was both a warrior deity and an agricultural god. In Roman tradition, a horse race was held on the god's day, 14 March. Near Red Horse Hill are Spring and Sunrising Hills, and the Angles – who colonized the Tysoe area in c. 600 CE – held their festivals at the vernal equinox,

21 March.[14] So it is quite possible that the original Red Horse of Tysoe dates back to the 7th century.

Marking the land

The meanings of the British geoglyphs are complex and probably varied, and it might seem an exaggeration to claim a single hill figure as comprising a sacred geography. But the point about hill figures is that they can be seen for many kilometres. As scholar Gina Barnes has commented, 'the sphere of power of such images is defined not by the locus in which they reside but also by the viewing distance'.[15] She was talking about giant cliff sculptures of the Buddha in eastern Asia, but the same principle applies to chalk hill figures.

In the Americas, the meanings of all the ground markings described in this chapter have to lie within the religious and spiritual beliefs that held sway in remote antiquity. The basic association with shamanism seems secure, but the different types of markings naturally had different meanings. We are unlikely ever to understand these in detailed cultural contexts, but, in broad terms, ethnological evidence suggests that at least some of the abstract lines and patterns were types of magical landscapes. The effigies probably covered a range of meanings in varying contexts, so there were clan and totemic images, but also images of power animals or shamanic familiars, and the half-human, half-bird-or-animal imagery is almost certainly shamanic in nature, because key characteristics of the trance states experienced by ecstatic practitioners, especially hallucinogen-induced trance states, are the sensations of transforming into a bird or animal and of soul flight. In some cases, the markings appear to have been connected to ritual activity such as ceremonial dancing, or vision-quest activities. Whatever their functions, the ground markings represent, in one way or another, the direct mapping of mindscapes.

MAPPING THE MONUMENTS
Sacred Relationships with Land and Sky

Mapping mindscapes directly onto the land in one way or another was gradually supplanted in some cultures by the building of artificial sacred places – what today we call 'monuments'. It was the ages-old story of humankind trying to 'improve on nature'. But initially these monuments had to create a cartography of meaning for themselves; they had to create their own sacred geography. This was done by the considered placing of such structures: location was important and not some haphazard undertaking.

Placing was typically made with regard either to landscape in terms of topography or other monuments, or to the skyscape: the behaviour of celestial bodies. And sometimes to both simultaneously.

Monuments in the landscape

The landscape relationships involved natural places such as mountains or other topographical features that had been venerated in previous generations (see pages 10–23), or alignments or patterns with other monuments. There are many examples of this, but we will look at just an illustrative range here in these pages.

Stonehenge

The Stonehenge bluestones were sourced in the Preseli Hills of south-west Wales, where Christopher Tilley of University College London found that Neolithic monuments were situated in the same areas as those favoured by mobile groups of hunter-gatherers of the earlier Mesolithic era. Among many of the megalithic monuments that Tilley studied in the rugged terrain of the Preseli range was the Neolithic dolmen of Pentre Ifan. The craggy ridge of Carn Ingli rises dramatically on the skyline behind this monument. It is clearly noticeable how the slope of the dolmen's capstone exactly mirrors the angle of the Carn Ingli ridge: this might be accidental, but is much more likely to be a subtle acknowledgement of the original, natural, sacred place. 'The outcrops key the monuments into the landscape, drawing attention to their location and making them special places,' Tilley noted.[1] The natural outcrops were clearly sacred before the building of monuments began.

RIGHT **The capstone of a Neolithic dolmen on Pentre Ifan mirrors the angle of the Carn Ingli ridge on the skyline behind it, in an apparent nod to the natural, sacred place.**

Bodmin Moor

Tilley has also studied Stone Age geographies elsewhere. On Bodmin Moor in south-west England he observes that all 16 stone circles on the moor relate by sight, and sometimes proximity, to the moorland's naturally weathered rocky outcrops known as tors, where archeologists have found evidence of human visitation in Mesolithic times, some 7,000 years ago. Some circles are so positioned that they have very precise sightlines to distant tors. Tilley discovered that a shift in the placing of a monument by less than 30 metres (100 feet) would have obscured the related tor.[2] The placing of the monuments was accurate and deliberate. This is singularly true of the moor's most celebrated Stone Age site, the Hurlers, a triple stone-circle complex. It is so positioned that the weirdly weathered outcrop known as the Cheesewring is silhouetted on the skyline. Due to weather erosion, the litter of small rocks around the Cheesewring was arranged into a low wall or *teminos* (sacred boundary) in prehistory, quite probably before the Hurlers were erected. It is a natural place

that was considered sacred, and that connection was remembered and used by the builders of the Hurlers.

The Orkney Islands

Prior to the work of Tilley, monument-to-monument relationships were noticed in the Orkney group of islands off the north coast of Scotland. In 1983, David Fraser reported on his study of Bronze Age cairns there. He found such monuments on different islands to be sometimes visible one to another, as well as being intervisible within individual islands. 'Intervisibility is not a simple reflection of proximity,' he observed, 'and is influenced by subtle changes in the landscape.'[3] He found sightlines up to 18 km (11 miles) in length, and concluded that cairns that showed evidence of being special in one way or another were located in visually dominant places.

Cornwall

Another archeologist, Frances Peters, found that solitary standing stones (known as menhirs) scattered across the tip of the Cornish peninsula in extreme south-west

LEFT The Hurlers Stone Circle complex on Bodmin Moor in south west England is positioned so that the Cheesewring is silhouetted on the skyline beyond.

MONUMENTAL SCALE

Intervisibility of monuments could sanctify large swathes of landscape, as noted with regard to hill figures in the previous chapter (see page 105). In Afghanistan, as another example, the 7th-century Bamiyan Buddhas – 50 metres (165 feet) and 35 metres (114 feet) tall respectively, which were destroyed by the Taliban in 2001 – were carved out of sandstone cliffs where they stood in niches and were decorated in dazzling gold.[6] As a consequence, they could be seen for kilometres, stamping Buddhist geography on the land. Gina Barnes has noted that such large-scale outdoor rock carvings on cliff walls or mountain boulders from Afghanistan, northern China and Korea 'forever changed the visible landscape at that point from a natural to an anthropogenic one with specific symbolic content'.[7]

geographical centre of the island of Java, clearly identifying it as an *omphalos*, a sacred centre (see page 43). Looking south from the temple, a mountain range on the horizon creates the visual resemblance to a supine person, whom legend states is the architect of the temple (see page 29).

But Borobudur is also involved in a third sort of sacred geography in the form of an alignment with two other temples some distance to the east – Pawon and Mendut. 'A straight line can be drawn from Candi Borobudur through Candi Pawon to Candi Mendut,' the Indonesian architect Soekmono observes. 'Moreover these three monuments are the only Buddhistic temples within a five-kilometre radius from Borobudur.'[8] That this is not, therefore, an accidental arrangement is further supported by local tradition, which states that the three temples were connected by a covered passage for religious processions. Such a procession is still performed, with the participants starting out from the Mendut end of the line. A pathway links Mendut to Pawon on the alignment, and an approach avenue to Borobudur has been constructed on the course of the line. There is also the site of a no-longer-extant fourth temple that fell on the alignment.

England were precisely intervisible, often at the limits of visibility over considerable distances.[4] She concluded that the stones had been purposely positioned along contours, perhaps marking out prehistoric boundaries. 'None of this would exclude a ritual function,' she remarks.[5]

Temple topography

If we look to Borobudur on Java, we can see that the 1,300-year-old Buddhist temple is a marker in multiple sacred geographies. Its site, formerly a Hindu holy place and probably an indigenous sacred spot before that, is located in the

Patterns of faith

The creation of sacred geographies by means of the location of places of worship

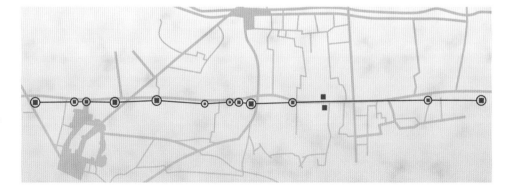

was not limited only to prehistoric examples – among other major religions, Christianity and Islam have been known to practise a similar art. It is well established that churches were sometimes built on earlier pagan (often prehistoric) sites in order to Christianize them, and even the Vatican in Rome stands on a pagan site. Geographical positioning was deemed to be important. In medieval times, more complex placing occurred – churches in old German towns, for instance, were often laid out to form the configuration of a cross on the urban landscape, and in York, England, there is a dramatic alignment running through the city involving seven ancient churches, including York Minster.[9] There are numerous examples of other alignments of ancient churches elsewhere.

Alignments of mosques also occurred. A good example is to be found in Cairo, where the mosque of Khalif al Hakim stands at one end of an alignment extending a couple of kilometres south-west to the mosque of Sheykhu. A total of 11 anciently founded mosques plus some Islamic tombs fall on the line.

In Istanbul there is a noteworthy multi-faith alignment of mosques and churches, first commented on by architect Patrick Horsbrugh. It is not even 2 km (1 mile) long, largely within the ancient town walls, and is marked out with evolved sites. The southernmost point is Sultan Ahmet Camii, the 'Blue Mosque' – so called because of the colour of some of its interior wall tiles. Built in the 17th century on earlier sites, it is apparently the only mosque in Turkey with six minarets and contains a piece of the Black Stone, the probably meteoric rock the main part of which is embedded in a corner of the Ka'ba in Mecca (see page 64). The next site is Hagia Sophia, over a thousand years older than the Blue Mosque, having been built in the 6th century for the Emperor Justinian as a church. When the 15th-century Ottoman sultan, Mehmet the Conqueror, claimed the place for Islam, he cast soil on his head in humility before entering the magnificent building, now a museum. The next site is Hagia Irene, also built by Justinian as a church, on the site of an older church. The immediately following site is the Topkapi Palace, which Mehmet the Conqueror built and which the 16th-century Ottoman sultan Suleyman ('the Magnificent') added to. This complex of buildings includes small mosques and the holy of holies, the Hirka-i Saadet, the Suite of the Felicitous Cloak, containing a relic of the Prophet. This alignment on the tip of land bordering the Bosphorus represents an axis that was respected for more than 1,500 years.

ABOVE **The Blue Mosque in Istanbul forms a multi-faith alignment with the Hagia Sophia, Hagia Irene and the Topkapi Palace.**

Heaven on Earth

There are many hundreds of sacred sites that are claimed to be oriented to significant astronomical directions, such as midsummer, midwinter and equinoctial sun risings and settings, as well as lunar, planetary and stellar rise and set points – all testifying to the care with which ancient builders positioned their monuments.

ABOVE **Vijayanagara in Karnataka, India was laid out as a mandala. The city aligns with a temple on a nearby hill, above which the pole star, considered to be the 'Pillar of the Sky', shines directly.**

But there are also examples where observance of skylore involved topographical elements or relationships between monuments, creating a hybrid heaven-on-earth sacred geography extending beyond single sites. It is those cases that are more relevant in the context of this book.

Star cities

Vijayanagara ('Victory City'), set in granite country in Karnataka, India, was the holy capital of a great Hindu empire that at its height in the 16th century ruled over much of southern India. Today it is a complex of ruins covering almost 26 square km (10 square miles) and is often referred to as

Hampi, the name of an inhabited village at the site. There are major and minor temples in and around Hampi, and festivals are still held there. The city plan was laid out as a mandala – a meditational device involving a square or circular pattern with a central point, used in various Indian and Tibetan religious traditions, and also used for laying out temple ground plans. Astrophysicist John McKim Malville found that the main axis of the city aligned to the nearby hill of Matanga, crowned by the Virabhadra Temple. Moreover, he discovered that the pole star, Polaris, shone above the temple.

This star – the north celestial pole around which all other stars as well as their constellations seem to revolve as viewed from Earth, and which never sets in the northern hemisphere – was considered by a great many cultures as the 'Nail Star', 'The Pillar of the Sky', and so forth. It will be recalled that Siberian shamans in trance felt that their spirits could float up to Polaris with the smoke issuing out of their tent's smoke hole (see page 49). It was the central axis, the *omphalos*, of the universe to northern peoples. In Hindu mythology the pole star is said to shine above the world mountain, Mount Meru. All these images are related to the idea of a world centre (see pages 38–49). At Vijayanagara, this mythical arrangement was, in effect, made visible. The further north you are located, the nearer the zenith the pole star appears to be; at the equator, it coincides with the horizon. At the latitude of Vijayanagara, Malville found that he could look along the city's axis to Matanga Hill, its temple and the star all in one sightline, as Polaris was low in the sky. He remarked that 'the conjunction of celestial pole and sacred mountain could not be more clearly presented nor more dramatic'.[10]

Something akin to this cosmological plan operated in China, where the emperor ruled from the Forbidden City, which symbolized the pole star, his throne being placed on a meridian line marked on the ground as a straight marbled pathway.

Other star-struck ancient cities include Mohenjo Daro, one of the major cities of the Indus civilization of the third and second millennia BCE, situated in Sind in modern Pakistan. The axes of certain streets in this now-ruined city were aligned to the positions that specific fixed stars occupied at the time, while half the world away in Teotihuacan, Mexico, the entire street grid is laid out with reference to the star cluster known as the Pleiades.

Teotihuacan

This now-ruined ceremonial city was constructed by an unknown people some 2,000 years ago. Its temples, shrines, plazas and dwellings covered some 26 square km (10 square miles). What was originally taken to be its main north–south axis was a great road now referred to as the Street of the Dead, which leads to the impressive Pyramid

LEFT Surveyors' bench marks found on rocks and in buildings in Teotihuacan ensured that the significant astronomical alignment of the city was not forgotten.

ABOVE The Pyramid of the Sun in the 2000-year-old city of Teotihuacan, as viewed from the summit of the Pyramid of the Moon. The road is the Street of the Dead, which has a slightly skewed north-south alignment, due to the city's overall orientation to the setting point of the Pleiades constellation.

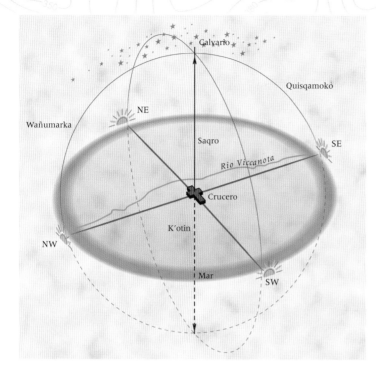

Calvario

Quisqamokó

NE

Wañumarka

Saqro

SE

Rio Vilcanota

Crucero

K'otin

NW

Mar

SW

ABOVE The sacred geography of the Andean villlage of Misminay is intricately entwined with the Milky Way, the concept of a cosmic river and with nearby sacred mountains.

over it, set to the same orientation. It was this astronomically significant line that had set the ground plan of the whole city, not the Street of the Dead, which had simply been set at right angles to the Pleiades line. Surveyor's 'bench marks' were found pecked on rocks and the floors of buildings, ensuring that the crucial alignment would not be forgotten or lost.

A river of stars

In the thin air and clear night skies of the high Andes, the Milky Way presents a vivid spectacle of diffused starlight. The Milky Way rings the celestial sphere, so when half of it is visible in the sky, the other half is hidden beneath the horizon. Its plane is at right angles to that of the Earth's rotation, which makes it appear to 'swing' in the heavens. It rises from the east to span the sky, and when its course passes through the zenith it creates a diagonal, intercardinal line – say, north-west–south-east; 12 hours later, after the Earth has rotated, the other half of the Milky Way appears and passes through the zenith, though now it cuts an angle in the other intercardinal direction, in this example, north-east–south-west. This celestial X-pattern has impressed itself on the cosmological direction system of the Andean peoples, who traditionally relate to an intercardinal quartering of the world.

In the Andean village of Misminay, two paths on intercardinal courses cross each other at a point in the village marked by a small chapel and known as the Crucero, 'cross'. This mirrors the Milky Way's apparent intersection, which is referred to as Cruz Calvario, 'the cross of Calvary' (reflecting the thin veneer of Christianization of the old Andean cosmological system) – on earth, as in heaven. One of the two paths links places at much the same altitude as Misminay, while the other path, Hatun Raki Calle ('path of the great division') goes down a slope. Symbolically, the two paths represent the

of the Moon at its northern end, slightly shorter than the 61-metre (200-foot) Pyramid of the Sun, which stands on the eastern side of the Street of the Dead.

However, the road is not a true north–south meridian, for it is skewed 15.5 degrees east of north, an angle that puzzled archeologists for years, until a cave was discovered by chance beneath the Pyramid of the Sun. Its lava-tube passage led into a four-lobed cave, which had been modified for ritual purposes (see page 17). This place had clearly been in use from a time before the city was built, and the really interesting finding was that the cave's entrance passage aligns to the setting point of the Pleiades, an important constellation in the religious skylore of most ancient Meso-American cultures. The builders of Teotihuacan had obviously placed great significance on the natural orientation of the cave, so it became a ritual place and, later, they built the Pyramid of the Sun

horizontal and the vertical respectively.[11] The village's irrigation canals follow the same pattern as the paths, running alongside them, carrying symbolism related to the indigenous conception of the Milky Way as a cosmic river.

The Crucero not only mirrors the heavens, but is also the centre of the village's sacred geography. Standing at the spot, it is possible to see the sacred mountains, the *apus*, on the skyline, where earth and sky meet.

Lunar symbolism

The midsummer sun settling into the breast of the Earth Mother goddess by setting into the Paps of Jura, Scotland – an event marked by the standings stones of Ballochroy – has already been noted (see page 34), but Scotland also offers a lunar mythological demonstration at the stones of Callanish on the Isle of Lewis in the Outer Hebrides. The Callanish complex seems to have been designed to mark the interaction between the moon and the local topography, when the moon reaches an extreme rising and setting position in its complex 18.6-year cycle, known as the major lunar standstill. (In the year of a major lunar standstill the rising point of the winter full-moon reaches its northernmost position, while the summer full-moonrise reaches its southernmost point. The elevation of the moon's arc across the sky in such a year also varies dramatically, so the moon can appear high overhead one month, yet seem to just clear the horizon another month.)

At this time at the latitude of Callanish, the moon rises just far enough to skim along the horizon to its setting point. It appears to rise out of the Pairc Hills, which, from the area of the Callanish sites, resemble the form of a woman reclining on her back. Sometimes called the 'Sleeping Beauty', her Gaelic name is Cailleach na Mointeach, the 'Old Woman of the Moors', a pseudonym for the Hag or Earth Mother. She is well known to the present inhabitants of the Callanish area and was doubtless so to their distant ancestors. The moon then rolls along the horizon, passing

BELOW **The stones of Callanish on the Isle of Lewis were built to mark the interaction of the moon and the local topography.**

up the body of the Sleeping Beauty and finally setting into the Clisham range on a nearby island. But what is seen by an observer standing at the end of the avenue of stones at the main Callanish site is the moon setting within the tall stones of the central circle there. It would seem probable, then, that every 18.6 years in its great cycle at Callanish, the moon is symbolically born out of the Earth Mother as portrayed by the simulacrum of the reclining figure, and then 'dies' into the stones. A kind of Neolithic mystery play.

Solar significance

An example of solar symbolism occurred at the Coricancha temple in Cuzco, Peru, capital of the former Inca empire. This temple was aligned to the midwinter, solstitial, rising sun (21 June in the southern hemisphere), and on that day the emperor – the Inca – would have sat in a special gold-plated and gem-encrusted niche awaiting the first sunbeams. When they shone into the recess they would have caused a glittering blaze of golden light enveloping the Inca, spectacularly confirming him as 'Son of the Sun'.

However, the symbolism did not end there. Radiating out from Cuzco are 41 *ceques*, 'virtual' lines linking sacred places

or *huacas*. These lines seem to have served a number of functions, but at least one was associated with a pilgrimage route that moved on a direct course from the sacred hill of Huanacauri, a little over 19 km (12 miles) from Cuzco, and outwards passing through 21 sacred places to the village of Vilcanota, 'sun house'. This particular *ceque* aligns to the midwinter sunrise position, and is also directed towards the Island of the Sun in Lake Titicaca more than 242 km (150 miles) further on. In Inca myth (and probably pre-Inca mythology, too), Lake Titicaca was seen as the birthplace of the sun and the place from which the Inca believed they originated. We do not know if the pilgrimage extended that far, but it may have done.

Ancient moonshine

A classic case of specifically lunar-associated sacred geography concerns the organization of the large Buddhist stupas in the Kathmandu Valley of Nepal, where the moon is associated with the religious calendar, the cultivation of rice and ritual activity. Researcher Reinhard Herdick has found that, with only one exception (Kirtipur, which has a solar, solstitial orientation), the orientation and positioning of all the large stupas can be linked with key moonrise directions.[12]

He worked out that the whole system in the Kathmandu Valley was surveyed from a flat-topped hillock with unobstructed eastward views. This is situated exactly midway between the major stupas of Svayambhu and Kirtipur, and seven alignments of stupas intersect at it. Almost all of the stupas are oriented to the moon in two ways: by the orientation of the stupa itself, and by means of alignments of two stupa buildings (or between a stupa and the hillock), establishing directional indications to points of lunar significance on the horizon. There are other, more subtle factors, too. A box-like superstructure (*harmika*) rests on top of each stupa dome, on which are painted the large eyes of the omnipresent Buddha. Herdick remarks that 'the intimation that the Buddha is looking towards a rising (or setting) heavenly body offers itself, as it is the actual direction of the gaze'. Also, the sizes of certain stupas varied in accord with the slight changes in the apparent width of the lunar disc at different points in its cycle.

The exact age of the lunar-based stupa geography in the Kathmandu Valley is not known, but lunar astronomy, calendars and worship go back to Vedic times in India (the 1st millennium BCE). In accord with other researchers, Herdick concludes that it was the sites that had initial significance, and the later stupas merely added to it. He sees the first, oldest work at the survey hillock as being the observation and systemization of astronomical behaviour. The next step was to bring 'the heavenly phenomena into relation with the earthly environment'. Finally there was the building of oriented shrine structures.

Another cluster of lunar-oriented sites, probably more ancient even than the Kathmandu case, is to be found in Aberdeenshire, north-east Scotland. The sites are known as 'recumbent' stone circles because each circle has a massive, altar-like horizontal stone placed in its ring of

otherwise upright stones. There has been archeological speculation that some of these circles are aligned to the moon at the 'major standstill' part of its 18.6-year cycle. Some of the recumbent circles may have been oriented to these extreme lunar positions for ceremonial effect, so when viewed from within one of the rings of stone, a major-standstill low moon would suddenly appear from behind one of the upright stones flanking the recumbent megalith and would seem to slowly 'roll' across the altar-like top of the horizontal stone, before disappearing behind the upright flanking stone at the other end. The recumbent stone and its flankers would therefore act much like a stage on which the moon made a dramatic appearance – ceremonial theatrics.

ABOVE Buddhist stupas in the Kathmandu valley of Nepal are oriented to the moon – a factor indicated by large painted eyes on the top of each stupa dome.

BELOW The Easter Aquorthies recumbent stone circle in Aberdeenshire is one of a cluster of recumbent stone circles in the area thought to have been aligned to the moon for ceremonial effect.

Stone Age sacred cosmology

It is fitting that the iconic (and World Heritage) Stone Age ritual landscapes of both Stonehenge and Avebury in Wiltshire, southern England, provide evidence of a fusion of monument, topographical and skyscape relationships.

The Stonehenge Riverside Project

An intensive archeological study of the Stonehenge landscape, called the Stonehenge Riverside Project, took place between 2003 and 2009.[13] A little more light has been shed on the sacred geography of the area as a result.

One of the first features constructed in the Stonehenge landscape was the Greater Stonehenge Cursus, which runs for almost 3 km (2 miles) across country a short distance north of where the stones of

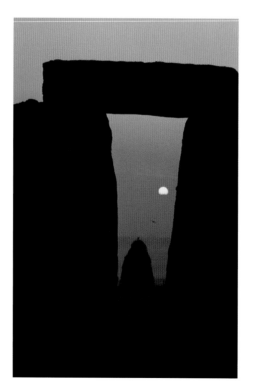

RIGHT **The Heel Stone at Stonehenge marks the alignment of the Avenue to the midsummer sunrise when viewed from within the stones at Stonehenge.**

Stonehenge now stand on Salisbury Plain. Excavation by the project found nothing within this great linear feature – it was a broad, empty line across the landscape, as has been the finding with other cursuses (see pages 84–85). This cursus, as others, remains a mystery. But major new findings resulted from the project's exploration of Durrington Walls, a huge henge monument about 3 km (2 miles) north-east of Stonehenge. This earthwork is 480 metres (1,575 feet) in diameter and is defined by a ditch 6 metres (20 feet) deep and 16 metres (52 feet) wide, edged by a bank 3 metres (10 feet) high. The archeologists found that it had contained settings of substantial timber posts, and that it had been a place for feasts by many people. There had also been huts for numerous dwellings. It was place for the living at least as much as for the dead. The project's excavators unearthed a highly engineered ritual causeway that led down to the nearby River Avon from the henge.

When the mosaic pieces of archeological findings were put together, a picture emerged of the place being used to celebrate the recent dead, and the river being used as a link with Stonehenge, a place of the ancestors. Along the river banks there was evidence of what may have been funeral pyres. It was thought that processions would have taken place along the river bank to the point where the Stonehenge Avenue led up from the river. People would have processed up this linear earthwork, the Avenue, which has a sharp

bend in it before Stonehenge is reached. As one turns this bend and walks onwards, Stonehenge suddenly and dramatically appears over a ridge. This latter segment of the Avenue runs straight to the monument.

The Avenue is aligned to the midsummer sunrise when viewed from within the ring of stones at Stonehenge, an event marked by the giant Heel Stone, which stands in the Avenue close to where it connects with the circular earthwork, the actual henge, surrounding the stones. Excavation by the project revealed something totally unexpected – linear runnels in the chalk surface beneath the Avenue. It transpired that these had been formed after the last Ice Age by water freezing and then melting. These natural runnels happened to align directly towards the midsummer sunrise. Mike Parker Pearson, leader of the Stonehenge Riverside Project, thinks that the builders of Stonehenge saw this and made use of it, probably considering that the ancestors were giving a sign as to where Stonehenge should be built. Actually, this

coincidence of nature is even more remarkable, because the runnels, monumentalized by the earthwork Avenue, also generally align to moonrise at the major lunar standstill. (It is increasingly being understood by researchers that Stonehenge was originally a lunar temple before it became a solar site.)

Stonehenge also has many other astronomical alignments built into it, notably those indicated by the corners of a huge rectangle marked by what are called the Station Stones, which sit between the henge earthwork and the ring of stones. Alignments between these four positions and diagonals across the rectangle that is created by using them yield directions to, variously, the midwinter sunrise, midwinter sunset, and moon risings and settings at midwinter and midsummer at both major- and minor-standstill times. Stonehenge is supremely well keyed into both its landscape and its skyscape, creating a true cosmological geography around itself.

ABOVE **The Station Stones at Stonehenge mark the four corners of a rectangle, within which the alignments are to various sun and moon risings and settings.**

Silbury Hill

The great Avebury complex, a bare 32 km (20 miles) north of Stonehenge, has an even deeper land–sky association. Avebury is a much larger henge monument than Stonehenge, enclosing more than 11 hectares (28 acres) and containing an outer ring of standing stones, which has further stone settings within its circumference. In the Neolithic landscape surrounding the henge is the West Kennet Avenue of standing stones running southwards, the virtually invisible remnants of the remains of Beckhampton Avenue running westwards from the henge, a multi-ringed feature known as the Sanctuary at the far end of the West Kennet Avenue, linear burial mounds like East Kennet and West Kennet long barrows, and, finally, Silbury Hill, Europe's tallest prehistoric earthwork. Because the shops, pub and museum are there, most visitors assume that the henge circle is the centre of the complex, but in fact it is Silbury Hill that lies at the hub of this great wheel of monuments.

Silbury is a flat-topped mound 40 metres (130 feet) tall that looks like a giant plum pudding. It has smooth, even sides, except for an eroded ledge running round about 5 metres (16 feet) below the summit. It has been excavated a number of times, but no burial or central chamber has ever been discovered. But turfs were found that were still green after nearly 5,000 years. They held the remnants of flying ants, indicating that the building of Silbury had started one long-ago summer around the end of July or early in August – Lammas in the Christian calendar, Lughnasa in the pagan Celtic one. Harvest time.

From whichever of the encircling monuments Silbury Hill is viewed, it is so positioned that the skyline behind it always appears to intersect its profile at the level of the top, summit-to-ledge segment. When viewed from the point where the tallest stone once stood within the henge, this top segment appears as if wedged between the distant horizon and the intervening slope of a natural ridge called Waden Hill in the foreground. Just before harvesting, around the time of year when Silbury began to be built, cereal crops on Waden obscure the view – it is a harvest-dependent sightline.[14]

Silbury was tightly positioned within the contours of the natural landscape. Finding the reason for this requires one to focus upon the riddle of why such a majestic mound was built immediately alongside Waden Hill, which is virtually the same height as itself. It turns out that in the late July–early August period, and in the early May period (Beltane in pagan Celtic tradition), when the sun rises along the same segment of the horizon, an observer on top of Silbury sees the sun rise first over the distant skyline and then, by going down to the ledge, witnesses it rising a second time a few minutes later over the top of Waden Hill. Silbury is thus built to exactly the right height, in precisely the right place, to visually separate the two (near and far) eastern horizons, allowing a celebratory 'double sunrise' at two key times of the ancient ceremonial and agricultural year.

There is an additional theatrical effect: a striking golden glow radiates westwards from the tip of Silbury's long shadow thrown by the rising sun. This is a 'glory' or 'Brocken's Spectre', an optical phenomenon created by the myriad prisms formed by dewdrops on the grass and crops in the fields to the west of the mound. When one is present at Silbury during this remarkable event, it feels as if the great mound is casting a blessing across the land.[15] In this role, Silbury is a harvest hill, and perhaps was seen as the representation of the Earth Mother goddess. Archeological investigators have dug deep into the mound over the centuries, even as recently as the 21st century, to find very little: no great burial, no British Tutankhamen-like tomb. This is, in my opinion, because the secret of Silbury is to be seen from without – exquisitely placed within the folds of the landscape and interacting with the rays of the rising sun.

Dark-moon rituals

The Stone Age sacred cartography at Avebury might not yet be totally revealed, because new research by Lionel Sims of the University of East London is indicating a strong lunar aspect as well.[16] After detailed field and computer research, he suspects that by viewing Silbury Hill from specific points marked monumentally in the complex, its top segment – if left as bare chalk without today's grass covering –

would offer a sliver of white glimpsed along the sightlines. This sliver, Sims argues, would have represented the crescent moon, rising and setting depending on the direction of view. This, he believes, was part of a system linked with 'dark-moon' rituals at the monument. 'Dark moons' occur when the moon is below the horizon, 'in the underworld', two days before the rising crescent of the new moon, and always happen in the week of the winter solstice (21 December). Sims believes that the Neolithic ritualists at Avebury combined a choreographed set of sightlines relating to Silbury with aspects of naked-eye horizon astronomy, in order to time a ritual at dark moon at the winter-solstice sunset.

The Avebury complex is yielding increasing evidence of having been a profound and subtle piece of Stone Age sacred, cosmological geography.

The sun of man

The early and medieval Christians were not above adopting celestial aspects of sacred geography from their pagan predecessors. Medieval monks routinely used the position of the sun and stars against skyline features and the roofs of monastery buildings to indicate times for prayers and observances.

RIGHT **The tiny chapel of St Michael at Rame Head, Cornwall, was oriented to a rocky outcrop out at sea which marked sunrise from the chapel on St Michael's Day.**

This practice seems to have existed from at least the 4th century in Europe, when it was used by John Cassian, who had acquired the method in the monasteries of Lower Egypt.

BELOW **This diagram illustrates the complex sacred geography surrounding St Lizier cathedral in France. (After Lebeuf, Brunet and Nadal.)**

Solar alignments in Britain

Medieval Christianity used celestial cues in other ways, too. Churches were supposedly oriented to sunrise on the festival day of the saint to whom they were dedicated. Though this does not seem to have been universally practised, and the procedure seems to have fallen out of use altogether at some undetermined date, a survey of 300 medieval British churches did show that a significant number were accurately aligned to sunrise on their patron saint's day.

It seems this practice could involve features in the landscape surrounding the church. So, for example, the very old St Piran's Church in Cornwall was oriented towards a prehistoric earthwork more than 3 km (2 miles) distant. Again, the cell-like 14th-century chapel of St Michael at Rame Head, Cornwall, is positioned on the top of a pyramidal hill and oriented to a conical rock outcrop called the Mewstones, rising out of the sea about 8 km (5 miles) away. These rocks marked sunrise from the position of the chapel on St Michael's Day (29 September) in the 14th century.

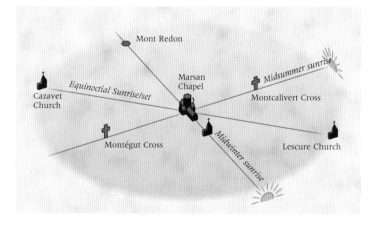

LEFT The sacred geography of the cathedral of Saint Lizier in France involves solar alignments.

European examples

Examples in France included churches that shared astronomical orientations with other churches in the vicinity. The medieval cathedral of Saint-Lizier, as an example of this, stands at the centre of its own sacred cartography. The central axis of the cathedral is equinoctial (east–west), marked out to the east by a church a little over 8 km (5 miles) away at Lescure, and to the west by the church at Cazavet, almost 8 km (5 miles) away. Two crosses positioned on either side of the cathedral create an alignment through the cathedral indicating the midsummer sunrise, while the midwinter sunrise is marked by an alignment involving Mount Redon a bare kilometre (½ mile) away to the north-west, the cathedral itself and Marsan chapel to the south-east.[17]

A more spectacular example is to be found in the Swiss Alps at the 15th-century church at Elm, beneath the Tschingelhorner mountain. A natural rock tunnel 18 metres (60 feet) wide pierces the peak. Local legend tells that the feature was created when St Martin hurled his staff after a giant who had stolen some of his sheep – and missed. Around the time of the equinoxes, the sun shines through St Martin's Hole and falls like a spotlight on Elm church, illuminating its spire for about two minutes. The sunbeam stretching from mountain to church is almost 5 km (3 miles) in length.

Although this phenomenon would have been occurring long before there was any church – before the time of Christ, in fact – it proves that church builders did seek out astronomical symbolism. This is further endorsed in that there are, apparently, four similar examples of this kind in the Swiss and Austrian Alps.[18]

Whether in Stone Age, Hindu, Christian, Buddhist, Islamic, Inca or other religious and cultural contexts, humanity initially sought to place its holy buildings within the frame of sacred mapping by careful positioning with regard to land and sky, earth and heaven. Sky and land met in the machinations of the human mind.

BELOW Around the time of the equinoxes the sun shines through the 'Martinsloch' in the Tschingelhorner mountain and falls directly on Elm church in the valley below.

SOUNDSCAPES
Listening to the Land

*M*ost sacred cartography was essentially visually based, but in
some cases there was the added dimension of sound. For
example, when working with indigenous communities in New
Guinea, the anthropologist Paul Wirz observed that the people's
sacred places had a distinctive acoustic quality to them, when not
distinguished by some visual peculiarity – especially swamps and
areas of gravel deposits, where 'curious noises' could be heard. These
were places inhabited by the *dema*, the mythical ancestors.[1]

Again, the prominent Rocky Mountain peak known as Ninaistakis to
the Blackfoot people produces sounds in the almost constant winds
that circulate around the peak: fissures and hollows in the rocky
summit towers form a kind of 'sound system' that produces a singing
noise. An individual at one of the numerous vision-quest sites near
the summit would have heard the mountain spirits singing to him.
As we shall discover in this chapter, there are many ways in which
the land can speak.

Voices of the rocks

Petroglyph Rock, near Peterborough in Ontario, is a large, sloping marble slab covered with several hundred ancient engravings – it is said to be the most-carved rock in the whole of Canada. Other exposed rock surfaces around it are devoid of such carvings, so why was that particular rock sought out as such a special place a thousand or more years ago?

ABOVE **Petroglyph Rock in Ontario is the most carved rock in Canada. It is thought that ground water deep below a fissure across the surface of the rock causes noises like whispering voices to be emitted.**

The answer most probably lies with a fissure about 5 metres (16 feet) deep that cuts across the rock's surface. Ground water sporadically flows along the bottom of the fissure, causing noises remarkably like whispering voices to issue forth. The tribespeople in this part of the Americas had a belief that spirits, which they called *manitous*, lived inside certain rocks and behind cliff-faces,[2] so voice-like sounds emerging from this rock would readily have been identified as the spirits speaking. It is easy to understand, therefore, why it became a sacred place,

perhaps even an oracle centre, thus accounting for the profusion of rock carvings on its surface.

Other rock-dwelling *manitous*

This belief in rock-dwelling spirits probably influenced the choice for the location of dozens of ancient rock paintings at another site in Ontario – namely Mazinaw Rock, which rises out of Mazinaw Lake and extends for almost 2 km (1 mile) at an average height of 30 metres (100 feet). The panels of rock paintings run along the base of the cliff a little above the water line; they were painted using red ochre (itself considered a sacred mineral), which is now somewhat faded. The imagery mainly consists of abstract markings, but interspersed among them are some figurative forms, including the large-eared jackrabbit spirit, Nanabush, and human-like beings in a canoe, usually the sign of spirits in Native American rock art. This site lies within Bon Echo Provincial Park, so named because the cliff-face produces remarkable echoes. (In summer, boat trips are given on the lake so that visitors can experience the power of the Mazinaw echoes.) The rock panels cluster where the echoes are strongest.

Algonquin shamans in trance considered that they could pass in spirit through rock surfaces to obtain 'rock medicine' or supernatural power from 'the men-within-the-rocks'. Indeed, this belief was held by many Native American peoples, and probably by other peoples around the world – it is known to have existed in southern Africa, for instance. The foot of cliffs that rise out of water, as at Mazinaw, was considered a favourite haunt of the rock *manitous*, which is interesting because such locations are also particularly effective in the propagation of echoes – the water surface acts as a kind of amplifier and transmitter. This was known thousands of kilometres away in Finland, as researchers discovered at three lakes in the Helsinki area: Nuuksionjärvi (the actual Swan Lake), Valkoinen-järvi (White Lake) and Vitträsk. Rocks displaying prehistoric carvings at the edges of these bodies of water were found to produce multiple echoes, and even echoes of echoes, especially when the sounds initiating them came from the lakes' surfaces.

Blowing stones

Rocks that could produce animal-like sounds probably had especially magical properties for hunters. One that fits this description is the Blowing Stone, to be found in southern England at the village of Kingston Lisle, in the Vale of the White Horse in Oxfordshire, east of Swindon. The rock is now no longer in precisely its original location, which was local, but is in an area rich in prehistoric monuments, including the Uffington White Horse hill figure (see page 102).

The Blowing Stone is a natural cube-like block of rock about 1 metre (3 feet) tall, pierced by several holes due to natural weathering or to vegetation growing into it over the centuries when it lay in the ground. One of these holes is the opening to a Y-shaped channel in the rock, and when blown into by someone proficient in playing wind instruments, it produces a sound alleged to be audible up to 10 km (6 miles) distant. It was described

in Thomas Hughes's *Tom Brown's Schooldays* as being a 'gruesome sound somewhere between a moan and a roar, sounding over the valley ... a ghost-like awful voice'. In fact, the sound is closely reminiscent of the bellow of a stag or elk, and would surely have been used in hunting rituals, or even to attract quarry in the surrounding landscape.

We moderns take sound for granted in our noisy world, but to ancient peoples who did not have a scientific model for sound, it could be magical.[3]

ABOVE **Mazinaw Rock in Bon Echo Provincial Park, Ontario, Canada, produces remarkable echoes. Panels of rock paintings along the base of the cliff suggest that Native Americans considered the place to harbour spirits and supernatural powers.**

Fairy music

Probably the most remarkable fact about rock acoustics is that some rocks, especially granitic ones, can produce musical sounds when struck with another, smaller rock. Referred to as lithophones, such rocks are not exactly uncommon in some geological contexts, but they are sufficiently unusual and remarkable to be noteworthy. To ancient peoples the sounds they produced must have seemed to be the music of the rock spirits, veritable fairy music.

ABOVE **Stalagmites in the Grotte de Clamouse, Languedoc, France, were found to produce musical sounds when struck.**

Stone Age origins

The use of lithophones dates back at least as far as the Paleolithic painted caves in France and Spain, those mysterious cavern systems whose walls were emblazoned tens of thousands of years ago with strange abstract markings and with images of bison, horses, sabre-toothed tigers, mammoth elephants and other creatures. It has been found that some of the stalactites, stalagmites and other calcite formations in these places produce musical sounds when struck lightly, sometimes even with a fingernail. The types of sounds produced range from pure bell-like ringing noises to melodious harp-like notes and gong-like tones.[4] Close examination of some of these calcite formations has revealed small-scale painted symbols and percussion marks so old that they have been overlaid with the calcite deposits of thousands of years. The subterranean sacred geographies of these Old Stone Age caverns had their own soundtracks, which we can still hear.

Stone Age usage of ringing and musical rocks is confirmed elsewhere. On the Karetski peninsula that pokes its rocky finger into the eastern side of Lake Onega, north of St Petersburg in Russia, there is a thick, flat rock that lies across a fissure that runs 10 metres (33 feet) down to the water. It is in an area of prehistoric rock carvings. When it is struck with a piece of wood, the slab or rock emits a low bass sound that can be heard right across the peninsula, a distance of well over 3 km (2 miles). Researchers think that the fissure or crack 'conducts the sound to the lake and onto the surface of the water'.[5] This in turn acts like an amplifier.

To take another example, at Balaphetrish on the Scottish island of Tiree, there is a granite boulder some 3 metres (10 feet) across that issues musical sounds when struck with a small hammerstone. It is a glacial erratic and is covered with prehistoric cup-mark engravings. It was clearly singled out thousands of years ago, and island people still make offerings at it in the form of coins deposited in a hollow at the top of the boulder. Other ringing rocks used in prehistory are known of elsewhere in Scotland, in France, in Greece and other European countries, and also in China, where ringing rocks were favoured for use in rock gardens (see page 147).

African rock gongs

It was probably in Africa that the greatest variety of lithophones was used culturally in prehistoric times. Examples are known of in Nigeria, Uganda, Tanzania, Kenya and Sudan; ethnographic information indicates their use in rites of passage, fertility or rain-making rituals, as signalling devices and even for entertainment.

The pioneer of African research was Bernard Fagg, who chronicled what he termed 'rock gongs' in the mid-20th century. He focused particularly on Nigeria. At Birnin

Kudu in Jigawa state, northern Nigeria, he found rock gongs clustered in the close vicinity of the Dutsen Abude caves, which contain Neolithic rock art. He experimented with tuning forks to establish that the rock gongs had been carefully selected from the surrounding 5-square-kilometres (2-square-miles) scatter of granite outcrops so that an organized series of sounds could be produced. He was also able to demonstrate that, with a little practice, local drummers could emulate the sounds of the full range of their tribal drums, including the hourglass-shaped 'talking drum' (*kalangu*), on the rock gongs.[6] Fagg discovered numerous other rock-gong sites in Nigeria, some of which were still in use.

Nile Valley examples

Rock gongs have been noted in the Sudanese Nile Valley, in particular from the Third and the Sixth Nile Cataracts, and more recently in several parts of the Fourth Cataract. German researcher Cornelia Kleinitz studied the lithophones on Ishashi Island at the Fourth Cataract, ahead of flooding produced by the creation of the controversial Merowe Dam, which was inaugurated in 2009. She found 25 rock gongs and 17 complexes of them in the granitic landscape, showing various

ABOVE Gong Rock, a Maasai ceremonial rock in the Serengeti, is an example of a prehistoric lithophone in Africa. These were used for numerous rites and rituals, as signalling devices and for entertainment.

LEFT The Balaphetrish Ringing Rock, on the Scottish island of Tiree, issues musical sounds when struck with another stone. It is decorated by dozens of cup markings.

considers that 'not only rhythms, but proper melodies may have been played'. Noting that the current inhabitants of the area now know nothing about the origins or purposes of lithophones, she aptly observes that 'the soundscape of Ishashi thus went out of use well before the modern era'.[8]

It might be that knowledge of ringing granite found greater sophistication further down the Nile in the later era of ancient Egypt. For instance, there is a fallen obelisk in the great temple complex of Karnak in Luxor. If the ear is placed close to the pyramidal point and the block is struck with the hand, the whole piece of granite can be heard to resonate. The German poet Johann Wolfgang von Goethe referred to architecture as 'frozen music', and so it seems to have been in ancient Egypt. Did the temples of the Nile have their own notes, their own sonic frequencies?

Other ancient lithophones

In ancient Greece such phenomena were certainly noted, as the travel writer, Pausanias, indicated in the 2nd century CE. He reported on the belief of the citizens of the city of Megara in Attica, Greece, that the god Apollo helped to build the walls of the acropolis there. In order to free his hands, Apollo laid his lyre down on a stone. Ever since, 'if anyone chances to hit the stone with a pebble, it sounds exactly like a lyre that is struck', Pausanias reported.[9]

Hints abound indicating that the knowledge and usage of lithophones was widespread in the ancient world. Take the ancient, now-ruined city of Jeresh in Jordan, a place occupied since Neolithic times. Amidst its paved and colonnaded streets, plazas, towers and gates there is a set of lithophones. That these are not accidental inclusions is demonstrated by the fact that the tones they produce are scaled. However, nowhere was lithophonic sophistication more pronounced than in ancient India.

intensities of percussion markings. Kleinitz felt it to be likely that 'activities at the different rock gong phenomena had diverse motivations and were directed at different audiences'.[7] The lithophones were virtually all found in association with Neolithic carvings of cattle in the rock art of the area. Where carvings were actually on a lithophone, the tones produced by the rocks were of a notably bell-like nature. Because of the variety of tones that the various lithophones produced, Kleinitz

Indian musical stone pillars

In 2002, archeologist Nicole Boivin of Cambridge University and Ravi Korisettar of Karnataka University led an archeological team that rediscovered Neolithic rock art on the multi-peaked, granitic Kupgal Hill in the Bellary district of India's southern Deccan. There are hundreds of rock engravings, mainly of long-horned cattle, interspersed with some human figures. While studying and recording the imagery, the team was informed by local people that among the rock art there were rocks that made deep, gong-like noises when struck. This was demonstrated for the archeologists, who marvelled at the sounds the rocks produced.

What is most interesting, though, is that in the same district is Vijayanagara, the ancient ceremonial city referred to previously (see pages 112–113), and at least one of the temples there contains musical stone pillars erected thousands of years after the rock art on Kupgal Hill had been carved. A full acoustic survey of Vijayanagara, set as it is in granitic country, might possibly reveal that it was a veritable sacred soundscape.

It is certainly the case that other temples further afield in southern India (at least) possess musical stone pillars. The use of such temple lithophones reached a very high state of development, a whole technology of sound – this is shown by places like Nellaiyapper Temple in Tamil Nadu, where columns fashioned out of a single block of rock 1,400 years ago are able to issue the seven basic notes of classical Indian music when struck. Did a sophisticated acoustic technology using lithophones develop over thousands of years from the Neolithic era to the early medieval period in southern India?

Ringing rocks in the Americas

The use of lithophones was worldwide, so we can expect to find them in the Americas, too. And we do. In fact, it is where we find what is probably the only lithophone featured in a museum – the Bowers Museum in Santa Ana, California. There, the 7-tonne (7-ton) Bell Rock sits on a concrete plinth in the entrance courtyard. Hollows where percussion had taken place over unknown centuries are visible on its upper surface. The great granite boulder had been brought down from Bell Canyon many years ago after vandals had toppled it from its position perched on smaller rocks – like most lithophones, it needed space around it in order to resonate properly. Now it sits mute in the museum's grounds.

There are numerous other ringing rocks in southern California, perhaps the most remarkable one being at a remote vision-quest site in the Chuckwalla Mountains close to the border with Mexico. Here a slab of rock rings with a pure metallic sound when struck with a small stone, sounding more like a hammer hitting an anvil than the dull clunking noise one expects from rock striking rock. There is a 1,500-year-old glyph etched into the top surface of the slab: the lithophone was singled out and marked long, long ago. Its sound permeates the silence of the surrounding wilderness – as with intervisibility, a single object like this can define a whole area of land, creating a specific soundscape.

BELOW A rare example of a lithophone being displayed in a museum, the Bell Rock can be found in the Bowers Museum, California. The depressions on the surface relate to where the rock was struck with small hammerstones during rituals.

A soundscape for Stonehenge?

A research team from the Royal College of Art, London, is making a detailed audio-visual study of Mynydd Preseli, in Wales.[10] This upland is a rugged, wild tract punctuated by the looming, phantasmagorical forms of jumbled spotted-dolerite outcrops identified by petrological and geochemical analysis as the sources of at least some of the Stonehenge bluestones (the shorter stones at the monument).

It is known that during the Stone Age 'pieces of places' were circulated as relics, in which material from venerated natural locations was transported to other sites, often far away. These 'pieces' might be in the form of polished ritual hand-axes or as rocks or clay to add to monuments that were being built – for example, the quartz and granite at the mighty Newgrange Neolithic monument in Ireland was brought respectively from the Wicklow Hills some 97 km (60 miles) distant and from the Mourne Mountains to the north.

Bluestone 'pieces'

In the case of Stonehenge, suitable pillar-shaped bluestones were prised from the Preseli outcrops and transported to Salisbury Plain, as discussed earlier (see page 108). They were the first stones to be erected at the Stonehenge site, which already existed as an earthwork. The abiding mystery has been why these Preseli bluestones, weighing several tonnes apiece, were transported to Stonehenge. What power, what *mana* or charisma did they possess? In conducting their project, the Royal College of Art investigators may possibly have chanced upon an unexpected answer – the relevant area of Preseli, around a ridge called Carn Menyn where most of the outcrops cluster, turns out to be a soundscape.

The acoustic properties of the Carn Menyn area manifest in two ways, as lithophones and as exceptional echoes. Some of the spotted-dolerite rocks have been found to issue, variously, pure bell-like notes, tin-drum sounds or deep bass rumbles in the very outcrops from where the Stonehenge stones were extracted. This property of the Preseli stones had already been signalled by the indefatigable rock-gong hunter Bernard Fagg, who also noted that the name of a Preseli village, Maenclochog, was Welsh for 'ringing stones' or 'bell stones'. The place was so named because, instead of church bells, it had two rocks that rang like bells (the rocks were destroyed in the 18th century). Did the builders of Stonehenge believe, like the Native Americans and the Bushmen of southern Africa, or members of the indigenous Shinto religion in Japan, that spirits dwelled within rocks? Did they believe in spirits within the Preseli rocks producing fairy music? Was that what made the bluestones special? There is no doubt that the Preseli upland as a whole was already highly venerated, as is testified by the numerous megalithic monuments scattered through and around the hill range.

Fort of echoes

Echoes, the other element of the Carn Menyn soundscape, occur most strongly at the rocky hill known as Carn Alw. The hill is a natural outcrop, but was pressed into service as a fort in Iron Age times in the final centuries BCE. The Welsh name Alw can be translated as 'call', which might allude to the exceptional echoing characteristics of this 'fort of echoes', as it has been called. The Welsh term *carreg ateb* can be used to refer to echoes, and literally translated means 'stone (or rock) replies (or answers)'.

If we think cross-culturally, the possibility arises that the Preseli upland was viewed mythically as an ancestral land of origin by the Stonehenge people. The Huichol Indians in Mexico, as one comparison, make an annual pilgrimage to the Wirikutá plateau, their believed land of origin, and collect the mind-altering peyote cactus for ritual purposes (see page 69). It so happens that the Preseli hills are rich in liberty-cap or 'magic' psilocybin mushrooms. During ritualized altered states, the fairy music from the rocks or the disembodied voices emerging from the flank of Carn Alw would surely have taken on an even more spiritualized quality.

ABOVE **The author tests for lithophones on Carn Menyn during the Royal College of Art's audio-visual study of the Preseli hills, Wales. Night-time is favoured for its quieter conditions.**

OPPOSITE **Pillar-shaped bluestones were transported from Carn Menyn in the Preseli hills to Stonehenge in the Salisbury Plain. The builders of Stonehenge may have chosen stones from Carn Menyn because of its proliferation of lithophones and echoes.**

Interactive soundscapes

Some peoples worked with their sonic environment. Anthropologist Donald Tuzin witnessed a remarkable example of this when living with the Arapesh people of Papua New Guinea. He was particularly studying the men's secret cult known as the Tambaran.

ABOVE **The Arapesh people of Papua New Guinea fashioned musical instruments from hollow bamboo tubes, which, along with drums, whistles, pipes and bullroarers, created sounds that simulated the voices of the forest spirits.**

Arapesh amplifying tubes

The Tambaran had specially modified musical instruments, such as giant amplifying pipes made from hollow, open-ended bamboo tubes up to 4 metres (13 feet) long, bullroarers (objects that make an eerie whistling sound when swung rapidly through the air on the end of a cord), slit drums, whistles and pan pipes. These are used to create sounds that simulate voices; sounds in which a listener feels dream-like voices can be heard. These sounds are believed by the Arapesh to manifest the utterances of great spirits residing in the forest.

When 20 or 30 amplifying tubes are heard in the dark of the forest night, Tuzin confessed that they create the impression of 'a chillingly immense, almost human voice'.[11] The sound was so disturbing and powerful that Tuzin suspected that infrasound (sound vibrating so deeply that it is below the threshold of normal human hearing, but can be felt physically, if unconsciously, in some instances) was being produced that helped to create the supernatural sensation. This suspicion was strengthened when he noticed that the Tambaran men conducted their rituals at times when thunderstorms were active in the mountains 19 km (12 miles) away from Arapesh country. Thunder produces infrasound that can extend much further than its audible sound, and Tuzin realized that it would wash through Arapesh territory. He concluded that the infrasound produced by the instruments unites with and exploits 'the roar of the unheard thunderstorm'.

A coded soundscape

The Kaluli and Umeda people, also in Papua New Guinea, believe the birdsong coming out of the dense jungle foliage to be the voices of the ancestors, that the living birds are giving voice to the spirits of the dead. They classify birds not by their plumage or appearance, but by the songs they produce. Anthropologist Alfred Gell came to realize that peoples who live in dense forests tended to have acoustic cultures, and made hearing

and, in some cases, smell the primary senses, ahead of vision. (The Kaluli even have a verb, *dabuma*, that melds the taking in of sensory information by ear or nose.)

Gell observed that the Kalulis' spirit idea about birdsong was only one kind of 'coding of acoustic experience': the sounds produced by rivers, streams, waterfalls and other environmental sounds enter the language of these New Guinea people by means of onomatopoeia. The Kaluli can 'sing places' like waterfalls, navigating a sonic cartography. 'Place, sound and social memory are fused together in Kaluli poetics,' Gell wrote.[12]

Speaking landscapes

The basic notion of the land having speech, or of being read like a text, was lodged deeply in some schools of Japanese Buddhism – in early medieval Shingon Esoteric Buddhism, founded by Kūkai, for instance. He likened the natural landscape around Chuzenji Temple and the lake at the foot of Mount Nantai to descriptions in the Buddhist scriptures of the Pure Land, the habitation of the buddhas. Kūkai considered that the landscape not only symbolized, but was also of the same essence as, the mind of the Buddha. Like the Buddha mind, the landscape spoke in

ABOVE The Kaluli people of Papua New Guinea have an acoustic culture, which puts hearing above sight. They believe birdsong coming out of the dense jungle foliage to be the voices of their ancestors and classify birds by the songs they produce.

ABOVE **The founder of Shingon Esoteric Buddhism considered that the landscape around the Chuzenji temple and Mount Nantai symbolized and was of the same essences as the mind of the Buddha.**

OPPOSITE **An Apache mother and her baby near Fort Apache, Arizona, 1873. The social behaviour of Western Apaches could be influenced by the names, stories or legends attached to many places on the reservation.**

a natural language, offering supernatural discourse. 'Thus, waves, pebbles, winds, and birds were the elementary and unconscious performers of the cosmic speech of buddhas and bodhisattvas,' explains scholar Allan Grapard.[13]

Mountain mystics in the Kunisaki peninsula, Kyushu, Japan, thought of the landscape there as being the topographical embodiment of the Lotus Sutra, a major Buddhist text. The peninsula's eight valleys were seen as landscape expressions of the eight scrolls of the scripture, 28 temples were built to correspond to the 28 chapters of the text, and it is said that as many statues were

erected as there are words in the Lotus Sutra. Walking in these mountains and listening to the natural sounds was considered to be the equivalent of reading the sutra.

Native American soundscapes

Other peoples also had some sense of the landscape communicating with them. One such society is that of the Western Apaches in the community of Cibecue, on the Fort Apache Indian Reservation, south-west of Flagstaff, Arizona. Keith Basso discovered that the names, stories or legends attached to many places on the reservation could inform the social behaviour of the people.

To the Apaches, the land 'stalked' the people, telling them tales to make them 'live right'. Basso noted that Apaches would repeat the name of a place two or three times because 'those names are good to say', and he sometimes heard Apaches reciting long lists of place-names quietly to themselves.[14]

For many ancient societies the land had a voice in their dreams. A clear account of this was provided by a Paiute called Hoavadunuki, who was a hundred years old by the time he was interviewed by ethnographers in the 1930s. The old Native American stated that a local peak, Birch Mountain, spoke to him in his dreams, urging him to become a shaman. The Paiute resisted, he said, because he did not want the pressures and problems that came with being a 'doctor'.[15] Communication from this mountain occurred a number of times throughout the man's life and was not seen as peculiar by him – indeed, the idea of the land being capable of speaking to humans was probably widespread in ancient sensibility. Soundscapes were simply a natural corollary of that sensibility.

TUVAN THROAT-SINGING

Another, different kind of example emphasizes just how broadly accepted the idea of communication with the land was. Throat-singers in Tuvan, an autonomous republic within the Russian Federation, developed their vocal art originally as a means of communicating with their natural environment, not for entertainment. Throat-singing involves the production of resonant sounds, overtones and whistles within the throat, nasal cavities, mouth and lips, and was used to provoke echoes or imitate natural sounds like waterfalls or wind. The master throat-singers can select precise locations inside caves where the resonances are exactly right to maximize the reverberations of their songs. They even wait until the atmospheric conditions are perfect for the greatest effect. It is in essence a technology of echoes.

At one locale, where a singer called Kaigal-ool performed in front of a cliff-face, ethnomusicologist Theodore Levin reported that 'the cliff and surrounding features sing back to the musician in what Kaigal-ool calls "a kind of meditation – a conversation that I have with nature"'.[16] Perhaps it is only in our modern culture that we have stopped speaking and listening to the land.

ENCHANTED GARDENS
Blessed Plots of Land

*T*he word 'garden' in English and many European languages derives from etymological roots meaning an enclosure. In antiquity, gardens were often conceived as miniature sacred landscapes, sequestered cartographies of the prevailing cultural mindscapes. In a sense, their setting apart from the actual landscape paralleled the movement away from natural venerated places in favour of monument building.

Garden history is a complex subject in its own right, so here we can touch on only a few key manifestations of gardens as sacred geography.

Ancient Egypt

Dynastic Egypt (c. 3000 – c. 350 BCE) seems to be where the idea of the culturally formalized garden arose, although there are hints of it in pre-dynastic times as well. A picture of Egyptian gardens has been built up from fragments of archeological material such as plant remnants unearthed in excavations, along with structural elements like garden walls and clay models of gardens. Valuable information has also been gathered from tomb paintings, along with texts on stone and papyrus.

ABOVE **Garden of a private estate with an ornamental pool, part of the wall painting from the Tomb of Nebamun, Thebes, New Kingdom, c.1350 BC.**

mortuary temple of Ramesses II on the western bank of the Nile near the Valley of the Kings (and the location of the fallen and broken colossus that Shelley refers to in his poem, 'Ozymandias'). Several gardens were located within the temple of Amun within the precinct of the great Karnak complex on the opposite bank of the Nile close to present-day Luxor. As well as gardens laid out under the command of the kings, some high-level courtiers and other officials of the kingdom also built 'gardens of the hereafter' for their own envisioned post-mortem existence.

The gardens were bounded by high plastered walls, and were formal and symmetrical to a considerable extent – twin groves, twin trees, twin pools, balanced geometrical arrangements of plants, and so forth. Terraces leading to different levels were very important. Gardens could contain lakes, canals or wells, gateways, pathways and steps, colonnades, pavilions, pergolas, small kiosk- or booth-like structures made from papyrus or reeds acting as shrines, retreats, birthing bowers or vantage points and sculpture – especially statues representing the gods, the king or the high-born person who had the garden constructed. At certain

Garden locations and layouts

There were gardens associated with pyramids (usually groves of trees) and other tombs, temples, cult centres, palaces and cities. In some cases, gardens were made inside temples (the atrium was an Egyptian invention), as is thought to have been the case at the Ramesseum – the times in temple or tomb gardens the statues of the gods, deceased divine king or other person were believed to actually come alive, in the sense that they magically embodied the living spirit of the represented being.

A basic garden layout might take the form of an entrance gateway (often elaborately decorated) in the enclosing garden wall, leading into an outer, open-air courtyard populated with trees, then a gateway leading into a second roofless courtyard with trees, then the whole centring on a pool or lake and buildings. But layout design varied depending on the type of garden involved. The reason that trees and terracing rising upwards from the entrance figured so strongly in sacred gardens was because they were echoing the Egyptian creation mythology, which was that the world was generated from a primal mound or hill that appeared out of a body of water – a primordial lake or cosmic sea.

Osiris associations

More specifically in tomb and temple gardens, the plan was based on the idea of the tomb of Osiris, the mythical first king of Egypt, who was mortal, but carried the seed of immortality (Horus) within him and symbolized resurrection in the afterlife.[1] Both the primal hill and the Osiris mound were believed to have had stepped slopes, hence the terracing in the gardens.

A key Osiris site was the Osireion at Abydos, built by Seti I (1306–1290 BCE) as his memorial tomb. This is now an exposed structure of massive granite blocks set in a sandy depression, but originally it had been covered by an earthen mound and encircled by six trees within a brick boundary wall. Remains from the deep pits in which the trees had been placed indicated that they were conifers and tamarisks. Tamarisks were symbolically related to the belief that the sky goddess Nut, who swallowed the sun at sunset and gave birth to it every morning,

also gave birth to a deceased king in the 'Field of Tamarisk' in the underworld. They also relate to the myth that Osiris was trapped in a cedar chest (explaining the conifer symbolism), which was then thrown into the Nile and eventually became washed up on the shores of Syria, where a giant tamarisk tree immediately grew. A further symbolic element was that Wepwawet, a jackal- or wolf-god who acted as a psychopomp leading the deceased into the underworld, emerged from a tamarisk bush.

Other sacred trees

Other key trees in Egyptian symbolism included the sycomore-fig, which was important for its fruit and medicinal properties, but was associated with tomb gardens because it represented Nut, the goddess who offered the deceased rebirth in the underworld. Sometimes the tree was also associated with Isis or Hathor, the Goddess of the Western Mountain (the Theban peak that overlooks the Valley of the Kings). The sycomore-fig was often used in avenues approaching tombs and temples.

The date-palm was another sacred tree, associated with Hathor. It was to be found

temple offering to the dead. Two species of the plant were known in ancient Egypt, the white and the blue – the latter (*Nymphaea caerulea*) has a perfume and is hallucinogenic; it is known to have been used ritually as part of the Osiris cult and for divination.[3] Papyrus of course had huge importance for writing material and many other uses, but symbolically it was associated with Hathor and the dead. In Egyptian art, Hathor was sometimes depicted as emerging out of the Western Mountain amid a clump of papyrus leaves to receive the newly deceased. Also in mythology, Isis hid the baby Horus in a papyrus clump.

Both water-lilies and papyrus were depicted on the capitals of columns in the halls of many New Kingdom (1550–1070 BCE) temples, creating in effect architectural gardens. In actual temple gardens, images of a god would be rowed in a boat on the miniature lakes as part of a ritual. Processions through the temples were therefore imitative journeys through a lake, in which model boats holding the image of whatever god was relevant were carried on the shoulders of priests processing through the temple, between the papyrus or lotus columns.

Numerous flowers and plants also grew around the garden pools or lakes. Among them were mandrake (which was used in divination), poppies and cornflowers (possibly associated with one of the manifestations of Osiris as the corn god). These and other flowers were found in the remnants of bouquets left by mourners. Sometimes temple columns were sculpted 'in the form of bouquets carefully constructed for presentation', informs scholar Alix Wilkinson.[4]

in several ancient Egyptian religious centres, and was the emblem of Upper Egypt. The doum-palm was sacred to the lunar deity, Thoth, and with its deep roots and liquid-bearing nuts was regarded as a source of refreshment for the dead. Incense-bearing trees like frankincense and myrrh were very important, and were believed to offer refuge for souls amid their foliage. However, such trees were not native to Egypt and had to be imported in order for cultivation of them to be attempted. The most famous expedition for these exotic plants was that despatched by Queen Hatshepsut to distant Punt in *c.* 1496 BCE.[2]

Water features

Pools or miniature lakes were vitally important garden features, often placed centrally, because, ultimately, they symbolized the primordial waters. In tomb and temple gardens they were usually rectangular or T-shaped, and the latter were particularly used as locations for offerings. Water-lilies ('lotus') and papyrus grew on the pools. The water-lily was prized as a

Akhenaten's garden precinct

One of the great kingly gardeners of Egypt was the heretic monarch Amenhotep IV (ruled 1353–1335 BCE), who changed his name to Akhenaten and, with his beautiful queen, Nefertiti, eschewed the pantheon of Egyptian gods (the *neterw*) and inaugurated a monotheistic religion based on the sun, the Aten. In compliance with what he claimed to be the direct command of the Aten, Akhenaten founded a new city, Akhetaten ('Horizon of the Aten'), now known as Amarna, in a rather desolate area on the eastern bank of the Nile that 'belonged to no previous god or goddess'.

Akhenaten created several gardens in the new sun city, the main one being the buttress-walled park, the Maru-Aten. This sacred precinct with was situated about 5 km (3 miles) south of the main city and contained two enclosures. The northern one was the larger, and in its centre area there was a sizeable artificial lake oriented east–west (the equinoctial alignment). The walls of the whole precinct were painted with images of trees and flowers. Entrance was via an elaborate gateway leading into the southern enclosure through a palm-pillared hall with carved reliefs. The southern enclosure also had an ornamental pool and, amid trees and shrubs, there were other buildings. A gateway in a wall led into the northern enclosure, one-third of whose area was taken up with the lake, a rectangular depression with rounded corners, which was 120 metres (395 feet) long, 60 metres (197 feet) wide and more than 1 metre (3 feet) deep. Trees ringed the lake.

On the eastern edge of the lake was a small temple, also oriented east–west, which contained green-painted columns decorated with water-lilies, together with modelled bunches of grapes and leaves. Adjacent to this temple was an island artificially created by an encircling shallow moat, symbolizing the mound rising amid the primordial waters. A shrine with an open court and other buildings stood on the island and were constructed from stone and precious metals. The floor of the shrine was made of alabaster and flower-decorated tiles, and paintings of plants and animals adorned the walls. North of the island there was a brick building housing 11 T-shaped offering pools.

The viewing place of the Aten

What rituals took place in the precinct are unknown, but Alix Wilkinson observes that the lake was 'large enough for processions of boats and even aquatic spectacles' to be performed.[5] The word *maru* has to do with seeing, and Wilkinson points out that the name of the place meant the 'Viewing Place of the Aten'. It may have acted as a ritual and ceremonial solar observatory.

Whatever the case, the splendour that was Akhetaten was destroyed and the king's heresy brought to an end. The sands of ages now blow across the ruins of the city of the sun and its gorgeous gardens, leaving only their remnants to remind us of when garden-making began.

LEFT View of the of the sunken garden of the northern section of the Harem Quarter of the Great Palace at Amarna.

Paradise

The basic history of the Persian garden is easily told. The first formal constructions seem to have been c. 550 BCE at the now-ruined temple complex at Pasargadae in south-west Iran. The gardens there were created by Cyrus I, founder of the Persian empire, who consolidated earlier garden concepts.

RIGHT **The garden at the Alhambra in Granada is a superb example of a Persian garden. Water channels reference the rivers of the Four Directions in the spiritual traditions of Persia.**

OPPOSITE **Elburz Mountains, northern Iran. The Persian visionary mindscape was projected onto their physical topography creating a 'psycho-geography'**

The Pasargadae complex boasted two palaces and two pavilions that were for viewing the gardens, because some Persian gardens were intended to be looked at rather than used. The gardens incorporated 900 metres (2,950 feet) of carved limestone water channels that fed pools at set intervals, and they contained trees, flowers and areas of grass. Persian gardens, which have a set range of geometric layouts (some more aesthetically rigorous than others), were also created by Darius, successor to Cyrus, at Persepolis, where there are bas-reliefs of plants and flowers. In the 7th century

Persia was conquered by the Arabs, who adopted the Persian garden, adding Islamic elements. Persian garden concepts spread far and wide, and so it is that we can see superb examples at the Taj Mahal in India and at the Alhambra in Granada, Spain.

Decoding the Persian garden

The esoteric meanings of the Persian gardens are a little more difficult to understand. The English word 'paradise' comes from the ancient Iranian *pairidaeza*, a walled garden. In terms of mythology, this goes back to the paradisal enclosure – the Var – of Yima, a god-figure of early Indo-European antiquity. The ancient Persian garden relates to a set of beliefs associated with a mystical and visionary geography that is alien to the modern Western mind.

In the spiritual traditions of Persia (ancient Iran), a fourfold body was envisaged for each person – a perishable physical body, an imperishable elemental body that operates in an 'interworld' state between the physical and the spiritual, plus two spiritual bodies, one of which is eternal. The physical body has the physical earth for its environment, while the subtler bodies exist in increasingly spiritualized versions of the earth. More accurately, each body projects its earth – what the late Henri Corbin, a great scholar of the mystical philosophies of the Middle East, called the *Imago Terrae*.[6] This mystical concept, so unfamiliar to our way of thinking, means that the distinction between inner and outer realities was merged. Yet more strangely, the earth was considered to be an angel, Zamyat, in the Zoroastrian system.[7] In the Avesta, the collation of Zoroastrian scriptures, we can find the statement that a liturgy is to be celebrated 'in Honour of the Earth which is an Angel'. Corbin referred to this Zoroastrian (or Mazdean) Sacrament of the earth as 'geosophy', literally 'Earth wisdom'. We think of landscape in horizontal terms (we refer to a picture that is wider than it is high as having a 'landscape format'), so this visionary world can be thought as a vertical dimension penetrating the physical world.

A Persian Eden

The centre or *omphalos* (see page 38) of this visionary mindscape was the Var of Yima, where the interworld is located.[8] The Var secretes a glorious light, Xvarnah,[9] and can be accessed in mystical rapture and visionary trance states, or at death. It is, of course, a version of Eden, the ultimate visionary garden. In its geography there is a central mountain that reaches to the stars and is the source of the waters of life, which flow as rivers in the four cardinal directions. Around the spring on the mountain that issues the waters grow plants, trees and flowers, including the all-white 'haoma', which can provide immortality.[10] Next to this mountain is another, the Mountain of the Dawns, made of ruby, which is the first to be lit by the rays of the sun. The third mountain is the Peak of Judgement, from which arches the perilous Chinvat Bridge, which souls of the deceased have to negotiate on their journey into the afterlife (or shamans and mystics in their trance journeys).

This visionary geography was projected onto their physical topography by the ancient Persians, creating what Corbin called a 'psycho-geography'. So the archetypal mountains of Yima's paradise were projected onto the Elburz range, the chain of peaks that stretch east–west across northern Iran. The mountains on the

skyline, around the edge of the world, were symbolically conceived as being buttresses against evil Ahrimanic forces, as well as expressions of the earth's urge to maintain contact with heaven.

The underlying layout of the Persian garden symbolizes the Var of Yima. The garden is quartered, usually by water channels, referencing the rivers of the Four Directions, and there is a central pool, referencing the spring on the World Mountain. This reflects the brilliant Iranian sunlight, symbolizing Xvarnah, the light of paradise, and can be used for focusing inner reflection as well.

Flower symbolism

There was also an ancient Persian system of flower symbolism, in which certain flowers corresponded to specific spiritual entities positioned on the spectrum of manifestation issuing forth from the godhead, the Light of Lights, down to the material world. Trees and plants, too, had their symbolism. So, for example, the palm tree represented the visionary earth and symbolized resurrection. The 'fruit that is Adam' sprang from a palm tree, one mystic sage, Abd Al-Karim Jili, asserted. He added, enigmatically, that the grove of palm trees is nowhere else but in Adam himself. The Qur'an also states that Jesus was born beneath a palm tree. The Persian garden was a holy scripture.

ABOVE An illustration of the Zoroastrian Eden, the Var of Yima, from 'The Chronology of Ancient Nations' by Al-Biruni, 1307 (gouache on paper)

The Pure Land and the Zen garden

*The minimalist rock and gravel 'dry landscape' (**karesansui**) of the fully fledged Japanese Zen garden, where water might be evoked without the use of water, seems a long way from the rich, paradisal gardens of ancient Egypt and Persia, but it derived from similar concepts, though of Daoist, Buddhist and Shinto origin, even if it ultimately came to eclipse previous concepts of a garden by eschewing symbolism in favour of the sparse, direct Zen way of thought concerning 'is-ness'*

Zen itself originated in China, as did the germinating sensibility behind Zen gardens. This latter was largely focused on rocks, an obsession that we can trace historically.

The special qualities of rocks

Imperial gardens in the Han Dynasty (206 BCE–220 CE) contained rocky islands in ponds, reflecting Daoist concepts of creation, which featured the idea of there having been floating Isles of the Immortals carried on the backs of turtles. These intermixed with Buddhist notions about a cosmic mountain, Sumeru, at the centre of the universe, surrounded by other mountains separated by oceans. Piles of rocks, sometimes reaching tens of metres in height, were built to represent Mount Sumeru. In response to another Buddhist influence, gardens were aimed at symbolizing the Western paradise, the Pure Land, of Amitabha Buddha (Amida Buddha in Japan).

In China, rocks were thought to be concentrations of the earth's energies, to harbour *chi* (*qi* in Japanese), the invisible animating force of the world, and rocks of unusual shapes or properties were considered to be especially endowed with this. Just being near to such powerful rocks could have a beneficial effect on a person's flow of *chi* and therefore his or her health and state of mind. Some rocks were bought and sold on account of their powerful qualities, and it was not unknown for someone to become awed and reverential when encountering an especially strong rock.

The scholar and poet Li Deyu built a celebrated rock garden near Luoyang, a major Chinese city and site of the first Buddhist temple in China. He used rocks selected from specific locations around the country, including Lake Tai, some distance west of Shanghai. Rocks from this lake were highly prized on two counts: they tended to be weirdly shaped, giving rise to simulacra of animal and human shapes, and they were often lithophones – ringing rocks (see page 128). When struck, they could give off a sound 'clearer than jasper chimes', as the poet Bai Juyi (722–846 CE) put it. Such lithophones were known as 'resonant rocks' (*bayinshi*), another example being the dark-grey, finely textured Lingbi rocks from Stone Chime Mountain in the Qinghsi range. 'The best Chinese rock will sound as well as look impressive when tapped,' art historian Françoise Berthier reports.[11] So some early Chinese rock gardens would have possessed an acoustic element; they would have been miniature soundscapes.[12]

Shinto influences

Buddhism reached Japan from China in the 6th century CE and with it the influence of Chinese culture and garden-making, though the veneration of rocks already existed in Japan, and had done from prehistoric times – there are hundreds of megalithic sites in Japan. Another influence that came to bear on Japanese gardens was Shinto, the existing indigenous nature religion, in which the forms of nature, including mountains and rocks, are conceived of as being inhabited by gods and spirits. According to the Shinto perspective, rocks in gardens should be unworked, and were sacred in their own right, whether or not they were part of a larger symbolical arrangement.

The word *niwa* means garden in Japanese, but it has a Shinto heritage in that it was originally applied to a cleared, sacred place where rituals were performed. The layout of a palace garden in Heian-period Japan (784–1185 CE) typically involved an open, spacious courtyard, surfaced with white sand, to the south of the main building, which would be linked to other key buildings by roofed corridors. Garden landscaping occurred around the courtyard's peripheries and would include a stream, carefully placed rocks and plantings (*senzai*). To the south of the courtyard was an irregularly shaped pond containing islands symbolizing the Isles of the Immortals, as in China. An arched bridge painted vermilion would reach from the edge of the courtyard area to the main island, while flat bridges would interconnect the islands themselves. The main island was landscaped with low mounds and plantings.

The courtyard was used for ritual observances and entertainment. There was

ABOVE **Shinto had a significant influence on Japanese gardens. Rocks were thought to be inhabited by spirits and remained unworked.**

OPPOSITE **Rock Garden at the Liu Garden in Suzhou, China. Rocks of unusual shapes were considered to be endowed with *chi*.**

WATER AND 'DRY LANDSCAPE'

Water in whatever form – springs, streams, waterfalls or miniature cascades – was a very important element for Heian-period gardens, whether religious or for pleasure. Although Heian gardens were essentially water gardens, dry-landscape areas were already known during that era, but the term 'dry landscape' (*karesansui*) first appears at the beginning of the 11th century in the *Sakuteiki*, the oldest manual of Japanese gardening to survive. It defines the term as meaning 'a place without pond or stream, where one arranges rocks'. The opening phrase of the *Sakuteiki*, 'When placing rocks...' eventually came to be synonymous with making gardens. This in time became the framework for the Zen garden.

a cycle of annual observances that commenced each year with the emperor invoking seven times the star of the year (one of the seven stars of Ursa Major, the Plough or Big Dipper constellation), and saluted the sky, the earth and the four cardinal directions.[13] Special rituals, such as invoking rain during times of drought, were also conducted when necessary.

Daoist concepts

Japanese gardens were influenced by Daoist thought, too. There was its concept of four mythic creatures guarding the four compass points: in the east the Green Dragon, which governed moving waters; in the south the Red Phoenix, which ruled over the lowlands; to the west the White Tiger, which governed the main highways; and to the north the Black Warrior (a tortoise wrapped around by a serpent), which ruled the peaks and uplands. So the ideal garden had to include a stream in the east, a hollow in the south, a path in the west or else seven maple trees in its stead, and a raised feature such as a mound or upright rock to the north (or three cypresses if that was not possible).

Shingon School of Esoteric Buddhism

Returning from an extended stay in China, the Japanese monk Kūkai introduced the Shingon School of Esoteric Buddhism to Japan at the beginning of the 9th century. This brought a strong Buddhist influence to bear on Japanese gardens, strengthening the 'Pure Land' paradisal aspect. The mandala format became popular, at least in spirit if not always strictly formally; rocks in waterfalls were seen as manifestations of the Buddhist pantheon of religious figures; and ponds came to symbolize the lotus pool in which the dead are reborn in the Pure Land. Seasonal plants and trees were favoured, as these expressed Buddhist ideas about the birth–death cycle.

Overall, the Japanese garden was 'informed by the greatest religious currents of East Asia'[14] and unified them. By the 9th century Japan was developing its own culture. Chinese themes were relegated as the Japanese landscape became a focus in literature, painting and garden landscaping.

Zen spirituality

Although Zen Buddhism arrived in Japan in the 8th century, its approach did not really start to become properly culturally transplanted until the late 12th century. Zen is a system of thought rather than a religion or philosophy. It is practical, in-your-face spirituality – it does not promote worship of gods or posit future heavenworlds, but focuses on the here and

now. It says that there is no state of spiritual enlightenment to be attained, as human beings are already enlightened – it is just that they do not know it. So the way of Zen aims at releasing us from our ignorance; it seeks to wake us up from our spiritual slumber.

As one Zen aphorism more or less puts it, there is but a split hair's difference between our non-enlightened and enlightened conditions, and if one can make that tiny but critical shift, 'what is gained is no gain, yet there is something truly gained in this'. (The *koan*, a rationality-evading, thought-stopping paradox or absurdity is a key tool in Zen; the most famous example is the question 'What is the sound of one hand clapping?') The enlightened person has lost the illusion of self, and can see the world as it is, in its 'is-ness', in its 'just-so' actuality, free of anthropocentricity, associations and all other chains of thought.

Musō Soseki's masterpieces

The father of the Zen garden was Musō Soseki. Although originally an adherent of Shingon Buddhism, he entered a Zen monastery in 1294. While he was there, Kyoto became the Japanese capital as it had been once before, ushering in the Monomachy period, which lasted until 1573.

In 1339, Soseki undertook the restoration of the Saihoji Temple garden, near Kyoto. This had originally been an Amida Pure Land paradisal garden, but Soseki made striking changes to it. More significantly, though, he created a second garden at the temple. A gate north of the pond in the first garden and some stone steps lead up into a sloping area of large rocks and trees, utterly different from the lower garden. The rocks seem to have tumbled down the slope naturally from among the trees, but in fact they were carefully placed by Soseki. This dry garden offers a raw spectacle that represented a stark break with earlier conventions. Soseki had, in fact, made use of some partially dressed rocks from a nearby prehistoric burial site, which may have been a curious way of keeping in with a Buddhist notion that funerary sites were acceptable as places of ascetic practice. Only monks were admitted to this second garden.

ABOVE Musō Soseki, considered the father of the Zen garden, restored the Saihoji Temple garden near Kyoto in 1339. He also created a dry garden, which included a rock cascade.

The tumbled arrangement of rocks is a 'dry cascade', with the impression of water aided by vertical streaks and striations in some of the larger blocks. If contemplated alone and in silence, on a windless day, what seems to be an auditory hallucination can reportedly occur, in which 'the deafening roar of a waterfall that is not there' is occasionally heard.[15]

Soseki's other masterpiece is the Tenryū-ji Temple garden, Kyoto. Here, he had to refashion a pleasure garden that the relatively new temple had inherited. This meant that its purpose also had to be refashioned from one of amusement to one of contemplation. Soseki shortened the existing pond and removed the island in it, putting in rocks instead. Beyond the pond he built a 'fall' of rocks, a dry cascade that formed the centrepiece to the whole composition. To balance this, he made a

bridge of three long, flat flagstones butted end to end – the first of its kind in Japan. Near the culvert to the pond he placed a group of pointed rocks, evoking mountain peaks and a deep gorge, and he created a rock grouping in the lake near its shore – this had a tall pointed rock symbolizing Mount Sumeru, thus keeping echoes of the earlier Heian-period paradisal gardens. He also displayed an early example of the practice of *shakkei* – 'borrowed landscape' – in which features of the actual landscape surrounding a garden are brought selectively into the overall composition. In this case, it was the mountain of Arashiyama. He built a pavilion from which the garden as a whole was meant to be contemplated as if it were a scroll painting.

Ryōanji Temple

By the time he had finished, Soseki had built an austere, contemplative garden befitting a Zen monastery, though it still had not reached the peak expression of the Zen garden. That occurred around the very beginning of the 16th century in the form of the rock garden at the Ryōanji Temple in Kyoto. Created by an unknown designer, its rectangular space of carefully raked, pale-grey gravel recollects Shinto sacred ritual areas, and that is probably what the place was originally. The space is bounded on the west and south by a low wall topped with an angled, tiled roof. There is a whitewashed wall to the east, and a wooden veranda along the north side. Within the rectangular gravelled area 15 grey rocks of varying shapes and sizes are arranged in five groups.

The setting has the unexpected effect of emphasizing the sky overhead, with its changing moods. The rocks present no easy resemblance to mountains or a landscape, and any number of attempts to decode the meaning of the rock garden has been made. Do the rock groups represent the Daoist Isles of the Immortals? Does the raked gravel symbolize the cosmic ocean rippling

BELOW A plan of the garden of Ryōanji Temple shows the arrangement of the 15 grey rocks, the meaning of which remains elusive.

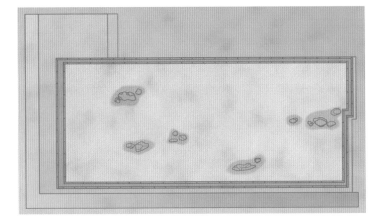

around them? Is there significance in the number or placing of the rocks? In truth, this mysterious garden whose main flower is emptiness offers no compromise; it is what it is. It is the pure expression of 'is-ness'.

Daisen-in

'All the Zen gardens that come after the one at Ryōanji are naturally a part of its legacy,' Berthier declares.[16] Among these is the roughly contemporary Daisen-in at Daitokuji Temple, Kyoto. In the east garden the allusion to water is strong, with current-like markings raked into the gravel and evocative placings of rock groupings. Two large rocks close together suggest a waterfall cleft in a mountain, from which a river can be fancied to run through a gorge and then to flow gracefully out onto a plain punctuated by hills. One small rock even looks like a boat navigating the waters. This arrangement of around a hundred rocks clearly represents a landscape, which in turn can be read as a metaphor for the journey through life. All this in an area of just 70 square metres (750 square feet). It is a masterpiece of *shukkei*, 'condensed landscape', the complement of *shakkei*, 'borrowed landscape'. This practice of Zen-garden design parallels the arts of *bonsai* and *bonseki* (miniature gardens made on a tray), which originated at around the same time.[17]

The south garden of Daisen-in is different again. It consists of a raked gravel surface that is empty except for two small, sharply conical mounds of gravel. Being at the south of the temple, it is clear that this garden evokes Shinto ritual space, in which cones of gravel are perceived as reservoirs of spiritual essence that can radiate their influence out to cleanse the space. The garden is minimalist to the point of profundity.

Among several other great Zen gardens is the 17th-century Shōdenji Temple garden, which displays the innovation of replacing rocks with azalea bushes tightly clipped into rounded shapes, growing starkly against the raked gravel surfaces. Attributed to the master gardener Kobori Enshū (1579–1647), the garden also offers a fine demonstration of borrowed landscape: the garden wall is of the appropriate height for Mount Hiei, one of the hills surrounding Kyoto, to be visible in the distance, integrating it into the contemplative scene of the garden as a whole.

Zen gardens are the perfect exemplars of sacred geography. They are topographical distillations of 'is-ness', and provide the optimum locations for practising *zazen*, seated meditation. 'The garden is my Zen master now, and it is your Zen master too,' stated the philosopher Nishitani Keiji,[18] and geography inside or outside a wall does not come more sacred than that.

BELOW **The Zen garden at Shōdenji temple in Kyoto is innovative in its replacement of rocks with tightly clipped azalea bushes.**

Afterword: Geographies of the soul

We have now seen a panorama of the many ways in which the human race in times before our own saw the world as in some way alive, enchanted, sentient and capable of communicating with us. This worldview is the essence of all sacred geographies, regardless of specific cultural beliefs and differences.

ABOVE **Planet Earth from space, along with its attendant satellite, the Moon. This blue, white and green jewel moving through the void is the precious sacred landscape on which we dwell.**

We may dismiss it as irrational and feel superior to our poor misguided ancestors, but let us pause – might we not benefit from changing our own worldview, in which the environment is considered non-sentient, inanimate, having value only with regard to our exploitation of it? Would we be in the current concatenation of environmental crises if we considered the world as sacred?

Centuries ago, the Zen monk Dōgon stated that the natural landscape was the body of the Buddha, that the world around us – the mountains, streams, rocks, the very land – could be read like a scripture and actually listened to, if we are in the right frame of mind. This may seem nonsensical, mere poetic licence to our modern way of thinking, but perhaps we need to put our heads outside the confines of our current worldview from time to time. In his wonderful essay *The Rediscovery of North America*, the nature writer Barry Lopez tells of how the tribespeople of Kenya taught him to sit in one place for hours at a time in order to learn something from the desert. He learned that he needed to pay attention to the land, to approach it 'by opening an intelligent conversation' with it. 'We will always be rewarded if we give the land credit for more than we imagine, and if we imagine it as being more complex even than language,' he advises.[1]

Whether we realize it or not, we all live in a sacred geography. It is called Earth, and it is past time that we regained the ability to map it with meaning. We cannot, and indeed should not, revert to the sacred geographies of ancient cultures, but they nevertheless contain a lesson, a fundamental wisdom, that we would be wise to heed: the mapping of the physical world needs to be integrated with the geography of the soul.

Notes

Introduction: Mindscapes

1 A. Ereira, *The Heart of the World*, London: Jonathan Cape, 1990.

2 C. Toren, *Mind, Materiality and History – Explorations in Fijian Ethnography*, London: Routledge, 1999.

3 P. Hage, 'Speculations on Pulawatese Mnemonic Structure', *Oceania* 49, 1978.

4 L. Lévy-Bruhl, *Primitive Mythology*, St Lucia: University of Queensland Press, 1935 (1983 edition).

5 A. P. Elkin, cited in ibid.

One: The Topography of Myth

1 R. Otto, *The Idea of the Holy*, Oxford: Oxford University Press, 1924.

2 M. Leenhardt, *Travaux et Mémoires*, Paris: University of Paris, 1932.

3 L. Lévy-Bruhl, *Primitive Mythology*, St Lucia: University of Queensland Press, 1935 (1983 edition).

4 Y. Ustinova, 'Cave Experiences and Ancient Greek Oracles', *Time & Mind* 2:3, (November) 2009.

5 O. V. Ovsyannikov and N. M. Terebikhin, 'Sacred Space in the Culture of the Arctic Regions', in D. Carmichael, J. Hubert, B. Reeves and A. Schanche (eds), *Sacred Sites, Sacred Places*, London: Routledge, 1994.

6 Professor Timothy Darvill, personal communication.

7 M. van de Guchte, 'The Inca Cognition of Landscape', in W. Ashmore and A. B. Knapp (eds), *Archaeologies of Landscape*, Oxford: Blackwell, 1999.

8 R. Bradley, F. Criado Boado and R. Fabregas Valcarce, 'Rock Art Research as Landscape Archaeology: A Pilot Study in Galicia, North-West Spain', *World Archaeology* 25:3, (February) 1994.

9 D. Whitley, *A Guide to Rock Art Sites*, Missoula: Mountain Press, 1996. See also D. Whitley, 'Archaeological Evidence for Conceptual Metaphors as Enduring Knowledge Structures', *Time & Mind* 1:1, (March) 2008.

10 A. Kolata, *Valley of the Spirits*, New York: John Wiley, 1996.

Two: Places with Faces

1 O. Pink, 'Spirit Ancestors in a Northern Aranda Horde Country', *Oceania* IV, 1933–34.

2 D. Theodoratus and F. Lapena, 'Wintu sacred geography of northern California', in D. Carmichael, J. Hubert, B. Reeves and A. Schanche (eds), *Sacred Sites, Sacred Places*, London: Routledge, 1994.

3 M. van de Guchte, 'The Inca Cognition of Landscape', in W. Ashmore and A. B. Knapp (eds), *Archaeologies of Landscape*, Oxford: Blackwell, 1999.

4 T. Huber, 'Putting the gnas back into gnas-kor: Rethinking Tibetan Buddhist Pilgrimage Practice', *The Tibet Journal* 19:2, 1994.

5 E. Stutchbury, 'Perceptions of Landscape in Karzha: "Sacred" Geography and the Tibetan System of "Geomancy"', *The Tibet Journal* 19:4, 1994.

6 Huber, op. cit.

7 G. Barnes, 'Buddhist Landscapes of East Asia', in Ashmore and Knapp, op. cit.

8 Ibid.

9 Soekmono, J. Dumarcay and J. G. de Casparis, *Borobudur – A Prayer in Stone*, London: Thames & Hudson, 1990.

10 V. Scully, *The Earth, the Temple, and the Gods*, New Haven and London: Yale University Press, 1979.

11 V. A. Donohue, 'The Goddess of the Theban Mountain', *Antiquity* 66:253, (December) 1992.

12 A. Ross, *The Pagan Celts*, London: Batsford, 1970 (1986 edition).

13 R. Bradley, *An Archaeology of Natural Places*, London: Routledge, 2000.

14 D. Clarke, 'The Hag's House', *The Ley Hunter* 120, 1994.

15 A. Ross, personal communication.

16 A. Burl, *Prehistoric Avebury*, New Haven and London: Yale University Press, 1979.

Three: Centre Place

1 A. Gulliford, *Sacred Objects and Sacred Places*, Boulder: University Press of Colorado, 2000.

2 J. E. Snead and R. W. Preucel, 'The Ideology of Settlement: Ancestral Keres Landscapes in the Northern Rio Grande', in W. Ashmore and A. B. Knapp (eds), *Archaeologies of Landscape*, Oxford: Blackwell, 1999.

3 D. Freidel, 'Centering the World', in D. Freidel, L. Schelke and J. Parker (eds), *Maya Cosmos*, New York: William Morrow, 1993.

4 J. G. Neihardt, *Black Elk Speaks*, New York: Washington Square Press, 1932 (1959 edition).

5 C. G. Jung, *On the Nature of the Psyche*, New York and Princeton: Princeton University Press (Bollingen Series), 1960.

Four: Walking through Holy Lands

1 E. V. Walter, *Placeways*, Chapel Hill, NC: University of North Carolina Press, 1988.

2 S. Coleman and J. Elsner, *Pilgrimage*, Cambridge, MA: Harvard University Press, 1995.

3 R. Loveday, 'Double Entrance Henges – Routes to the Past?', in A. Gibson and D. Simpson (eds), *Prehistoric Ritual and Religion*, Stroud: Sutton Publishing, 1998.

4 S. A. Takacs, 'Divine and Human Feet: Records of Pilgrims Honouring Isis', in J. Elsner and I. Rutherford (eds), *Pilgrimage in Graeco-Roman and Early Christian Antiquity*, Oxford: Oxford University Press, 2007.

5 N. Edwards, *The Archaeology of Early Medieval Ireland*, London: Batsford, 1990.

6 P. Harbison, 'Early Irish Pilgrim Archaeology in the Dingle Peninsula', *World Archaeology: The Archaeology of Pilgrimage* 26:1, 1994.

7 D. L. Eck, 'India's Tirthas: "Crossings" in Sacred Geography', *History of Religions* 20:4, 1981.

8 B. Shah, 'Braj: The Creation of Krishna's Landscape of Power and Pleasure and its Sixteenth-Century Construction through the Pilgrimage of the Groves', in M. Conan (ed.), *Sacred Gardens and Landscapes*, Washington, DC: Dumbarton Oaks Research Library, 2007.

9 S. Coleman and J. Elsner, 'The Pilgrim's Progress: Art, Architecture, and Ritual Movement at Sinai', *World Archaeology: The Archaeology of Pilgrimage* 26:1, 1994.

10 P. Yeoman, *Pilgrimage in Medieval Scotland*, London: Batsford, 1999.

11 W. Pullan, 'Mapping Time and Salvation', in G. Flood (ed.), *Mapping Invisible Worlds*, Edinburgh: Edinburgh University Press, 1993.

12 A. Gulliford, *Sacred Objects and Sacred Traditions*, Boulder: University Press of Colorado, 2000.
13 D. Whitley, *A Guide to Rock Art Sites: Southern California and Southern Nevada*, Missoula: Mountain Press Publishing, 1996.
14 A. Kolata, *Valley of the Spirits*, New York: John Wiley, 1996.

Five: Lines Drawn in the Land
1 The spelling 'Nazca' used to be applied to these features and to the town they are named for, but 'Nasca' is now the commonly adopted version.
2 Tony Morrison, *Pathways to the Gods – The Mystery of the Andes Lines*, Wilton: Michael Russell, 1978.
3 W. Denevan, 'Prehistoric roads and causeways of lowland tropical America', in C. D. Trombold (ed.), *Ancient Road Networks and Settlement Hierarchies in the New World*, Cambridge: Cambridge University Press, 1991.
4 C. D. Trombold, 'Causeways in the context of strategic planning in the La Quemada region, Zacatecas, Mexico', in ibid.
5 T. Sever, unpublished dissertation.
6 S. H. Lekson, *The Chaco Meridian*, Walnut Creek: Altamira Press, 1999.
7 Hosteen Beyal, cited in K. Frazier, *People of Chaco*, New York: W. W. Norton, 1986.
8 J. Hyslop, 'Observations about research on prehistoric roads in South America', in Trombold, op. cit.
9 A. Aveni, *Nasca – Eighth Wonder of the World?*, London: British Museum Press, 2000.
10 Ibid.
11 P. B. Clarkson, 'The Archeology of the Nazca Pampa, Peru: Environmental and Cultural Parameters', in A. Aveni (ed.), *The Lines of Nazca*, Philadelphia: The American Philosophical Society, 1990.
12 H. Silverman, 'The Early Nazca Pilgrimage Center of Cahuachi and the Nazca Lines: Anthropological and Archeological Perspectives', in ibid.
13 J. von Werlhof, *Spirits of the Earth*, El Centro: Imperial Valley College Museum, 1987.
14 P. Devereux, *The Long Trip – A Prehistory of Psychedelia*, New York: Penguin/Arkana, 1997.
15 R. Stone-Miller, *Art of the Andes: From Chavin to Inca*, London: Thames & Hudson, 1995.

16 M. Dobkin de Rios, 'Plant Hallucinogens, Out-of-Body Experiences and New World Monumental Earthworks', in B. M. Du Toit (ed.), *Drugs, Rituals, and Altered States of Consciousness*, Rotterdam: A. A. Balkema, 1977.
17 P. Devereux, *Shamanism and the Mystery Lines*, Slough: Foulsham/Quantum, 1993.
18 R. K. Siegel and L. J. West (eds), *Hallucinations*, New York: John Wiley, 1975.
19 L. Spier, *Yuman Tribes of the Gila River*, Chicago: University of Chicago Press, 1933.
20 T. Hoskinson, 'Saguero Wine, Ground Figures, and Power Mountains: Investigations at Sears Point, Arizona', in R. A. Williamson and C. R. Farrer (eds), *Earth and Sky*, Albuquerque: University of New Mexico Press, 1992.
21 R. Loveday, *Inscribed Across the Landscape: The Cursus Enigma*, Stroud: Tempus, 2006.
22 *Handwörterbuch des deutschen Aberglaubens*, Berlin: de Gruyters, 1933.
23 E. Wentz, *The Fairy-Faith in Celtic Countries*, Gerrards Cross: Colin Smyth, 1911 (1977 edition).
24 *A Midsummer Night's Dream*, act 5, scene 1, lines 368–71.
25 N. Caciola, 'Wraiths, Revenants and Ritual in Medieval Culture', *Past and Present* 152, 1996.
26 A fully referenced and greatly expanded account of this material can be found in P. Devereux, *Spirit Roads*, London: Collins & Brown, 2003 (2007 edition).

Six: Giants in the Earth
1 M. Reindel and G. A. Wagner, *New Technologies for Archaeology*, German Archeological Institute/Springer, 2009.
2 F. Joseph, 'The Candelabra of the Andes', *The Ancient American* 10, 1995.
3 David Whitley, personal communication.
4 J. von Werlhof, *Spirits of the Earth*, El Centro: Imperial Valley College Museum, 1987.
5 L. Spier, *Yuman Tribes of the Gila River*, New York: Dover Publications, 1933 (1978 edition).
6 Ibid.
7 David Whitley, personal communication.
8 D. Whitley, *A Guide to Rock Art Sites*, Missoula: Mountain Press, 1996.
9 P. Nabokov, *Indian Running*, Santa Fe: Ancient City Press, 1981.

10 R. A. Birmingham and L. E. Eisenberg, *Indian Mounds of Wisconsin*, Madison: University of Wisconsin Press, 2000.
11 Ibid.
12 Ibid.
13 P. Newman, *The Lost Gods of Albion*, Stroud: Wrens Park Publishing, 1997 (2000 edition).
14 Ibid.
15 G. L. Barnes, 'Buddhist Landscapes of East Asia', in W. Ashmore and A. B. Knapp (eds), *Archaeologies of Landscape*, Oxford: Blackwell, 1999.

Seven: Mapping the Monuments
1 C. Tilley, *A Phenomenology of Landscape*, Oxford: Berg, 1994.
2 C. Tilley, 'The powers of rocks: topography and monument construction on Bodmin Moor', *World Archaeology* 28:2, (October) 1996.
3 D. Fraser, 'Land and Society in Neolithic Orkney', *British Archaeological Reports* 117, part 2, 1983.
4 In all essentials, this had been noted earlier: J. Michell, *The Old Stones of Land's End*, London: Garnstone Press, 1974.
5 F. Peters, 'The possible use of West Penwith menhirs as boundary markers', *Cornish Archaeology* 29, 1990.
6 As part of research in 2008 for a mooted reconstruction project for the destroyed Buddha sculptures, a 19-metre (62-foot) 'sleeping Buddha' sculpture was unearthed at Bamiyan and dated to the 3rd century CE.
7 G. Barnes, 'Buddhist Landscapes of East Asia', in W. Ashmore and A. B. Knapp (eds), *Archaeologies of Landscape*, Oxford: Blackwell, 1999.
8 Soekmono et al., *Borobudur*, London: Thames & Hudson, 1990.
9 N. Pennick and P. Devereux, *Lines on the Landscape*, London: Robert Hale, 1989.
10 J. M. Malville and J. M. Fritz, 'Mapping the Sacred Geometry of Vijayanagara', in G. D. Flood (ed.), *Mapping Invisible Worlds*, Edinburgh: Edinburgh University Press, 1993.
11 G. Urton, *At the Crossroads of the Earth and the Sky*, Austin: University of Texas Press, 1988.
12 R. Herdick, 'Remarks on the Orientation of the Large Stupas in the Kathmandu Valley: A Discussion of Principles of Lunar Ordering', in C. Ramble and M. Brauern (eds), *Anthropology of Tibet and the Himalaya*, Zurich: Ethnological Museum of the University of Zurich, 1993.

13 www.shef.ac.uk/archaeology/research/stonehenge

14 P. Devereux, 'Three-dimensional aspects of apparent relationships between selected natural and artificial features within the topography of the Avebury Complex', *Antiquity* 65, (December) 1991.

15 P. Devereux, *The Sacred Place*, London: Cassell, 2000.

16 L. Sims, 'Entering, and returning from, the underworld: reconstituting Silbury Hill by combining quantified landscape phenomenology with archaeoastronomy', *Journal of the Royal Anthropological Institute* 15, 2009.

17 A. Lebeuf, J.-P. Brunet and R. Nadal, 'Un Observatoire Paléo-Astronomique à St-Lizier', *Archaeoastronomy* 3, 1983.

18 M. Bischof, 'Alpine Lightshows', *The Ley Hunter* 113, 1990.

Eight: Soundscapes

1 P. Wirz, cited in L. Lévy-Bruhl, *Primitive Mythology*, St Lucia: University of Queensland Press, 1935 (1983 edition).

2 G. Rajnovich, *Reading Rock Art – Interpreting the Indian Rock Paintings of the Canadian Shield*, Toronto: Natural Heritage/Natural History Inc., 1994.

3 The study of sound at archeological sites is developing into a new branch of archeology and is formally called 'archeoacoustics'.

4 L. Dams, 'Palaeolithic lithophones: descriptions and comparisons', *Oxford Journal of Archaeology* 4:1, 1985.

5 R. Lauhakangas, 'A Lithophonic Drum in Lake Onega', *Adoranten*, 1999.

6 B. Fagg, 'The Discovery of Multiple Rock Gongs in Nigeria', *Man* 56, (February) 1956.

7 C. Kleinitz, in D. Q. Fuller, *The Central Amri to Kirbekan Survey: A Preliminary Report on Excavations and Survey 2003–2004*, London: University of London, 2004.

8 Ibid.

9 *Pausanias Book 1: Attica*, 42.2.

10 The progress of this project, 'Landscape & Perception', which is ongoing at the time of writing, can be followed online at: www.landscape-perception.com.

11 D. Tuzin, 'Miraculous Voices: The Auditory Experience of Numinous Objects', *Current Anthropology* 25:5, 1984.

12 A. Gell, 'The Language of the Forest: Landscape and Phonological Iconism in Umeda', in E. Hirsch and M. O'Hanlon (eds), *The Anthropology of Landscape*, Oxford: Oxford University Press, 1995.

13 A. Grapard, 'Geosophia, Geognosis, and Geopiety: Orders of Significance in Japanese Representations of Space', in R. Friedland and D. Boden (eds), *Nowhere: Space, Time and Modernity*, Berkeley: University of California Press, 1994.

14 K. Basso, 'Stalking with Stories: Names, Places and Moral Narratives among the Western Apaches', in D. Halpern (ed.), *On Nature*, Berkeley: North Point Press, 1987. See also K. Basso, *Wisdom Sits in Places*, Albuquerque: University of New Mexico Press, 1996.

15 J. Steward, *Two Paiute Autobiographies*, Berkeley: University of California Press *Publications in American Archeology and Ethnology* series 33:5, 1934.

16 T. Levin and V. Suzukei, *Where Rivers and Mountains Sing: Sound, Music, and Nomadism in Tuva and Beyond*, Bloomington: Indiana University Press, 2006.

Nine: Enchanted Gardens

1 In myth, Osiris was betrayed, murdered and dismembered by his brother Seth, but became reconstituted through the efforts of his wife, Isis. Osiris is a multifaceted figure absorbing elements of numerous earlier gods, and aspects of the sun god. Egyptian kings believed that they became Osiris at death, because it was assumed that the king was divine.

2 It is not known exactly where the land that ancient Egyptians referred to as Punt was. There have been suggestions that it was in the Horn of Africa, or in Arabia.

3 C. Ratsch, *The Dictionary of Sacred and Magical Plants*, Bridport: Prism Press, 1992.

4 A. Wilkinson, *The Garden in Ancient Egypt*, London: Rubicon Press, 1998.

5 Ibid.

6 H. Corbin, *Spiritual Body and Celestial Earth*, London: I. B. Taurus, 1976 (1990 edition).

7 Zoroastrianism was an ancient Iranian religion named after its leading prophet, Zoroaster, who taught the worship of Ahura Mazda, the sole, uncreated creator of the universe. The term 'Zoroastrianism' is effectively interchangeable with 'Mazdaism'.

8 It should be understood that this is a greatly simplified version of much more extensive and complex concepts that need not concern us here. Corbin's books explain them in detail.

9 This calls to mind the words of the English poet William Wordsworth, who wrote: 'There was a time when meadow, grove and stream / The earth, and every common sight / To me did seem / Apparelled in celestial light / The glory and the freshness of a dream...' ('Intimations of Immortality from Recollections of Early Childhood', 1807). The poet complained that in his adulthood the perception of such glory had faded.

10 'Haoma' is etymologically linked with 'soma', the legendary sacramental, vision-inducing drink of the ancient Indo-Europeans referred to in the Rig Veda. Researchers have long argued as to what it actually was, and suggestions have ranged through various psychoactive plants and fungi, including the white-flowered *Peganum harmala* (Syrian rue) and the red-capped, white-spotted 'fairy toadstool', *Amanita muscaria* (fly agaric). For a full discussion, see P. Devereux, *The Long Trip – A Prehistory of Psychedelia*, New York: Penguin/Arkana, 1997/2007.

11 Corbin, op. cit.

12 F. Berthier, *Reading Zen in the Rocks*, Chicago: University of Chicago Press, 1989 (translation and additional essay by Graham Parkes).

13 This raises the question as to whether some of the later Japanese Zen gardens also have an unexplored acoustic dimension. Apparently the sound of a rock was less important to Japanese garden-makers, but they were still aware of such phenomena.

14 M. Vieillard-Baron, 'Religious and Lay Rituals in Japanese Gardens during the Heian Period', in M. Conan (ed.), *Sacred Gardens and Landscapes: Ritual and Agency*, Washington, DC: Dumbarton Oaks, 2007.

15 Berthier, op. cit.

16 Graham Parkes, in F. Berthier, op. cit.

17 Berthier, op. cit.

18 Ibid.

19 Nishitani Keiji (1900–1990) was a scholar of Japanese religious thought. This quote is cited in Graham Parkes's essay, op. cit.

Afterword

1 B. Lopez, *The Rediscovery of North America*, London: Vintage, 1990.

Index

Index/Acknowledgements

Author's acknowledgements

Because of its broad range of material, this book necessarily results from decades of field and library research, and I am beholden to large numbers of people who have assisted, guided and taught me over the years. Many of these people have been acknowledged in my previous works so here I will name only those who have provided me with new information or else alerted me to important sources that were relevant to this particular book. I therefore express my gratitude to Paul Allcoat, John Clarke, Charla Devereux, Jeremy Harte, Hans Kortekaas and Denise Wyatt, Shakti Maira, Marilyn Monk, and Natalie Tolbert. (Profound apologies to anyone I may have inadvertently missed out here.) I must make a special mention of Charla Devereux and Sol Devereux for accompanying me variously on fieldtrips, sometimes to challenging locations.

It has been a pleasure working with all the people I've been in contact with at Octopus Publishers/Gaia, especially editors Sandra Rigby and Lisa John, for unfailing encouragement and patience throughout. The picture researchers also deserve congratulations for so often being successful in tracking down some obscure images on my behalf, and I am grateful to the photographers whose pictures grace the pages of this volume.

Finally, I acknowledge the Arts and Humanities Research Council (UK) and the Lifebridge Foundation (USA) for grants that helped to make possible my visits to some of the sites in the Americas referred to in this book. I additionally wish to mention the Royal College of Art under whose auspices my colleague Jon Wozencroft and I have been conducting the audio-acoustic Landscape & Perception project.

Executive Editor Sandra Rigby
Senior Editor Lisa John
Executive Art Editor Penny Stock
Designer Janis Utton
Illustrator Sudden Impact Media
Production Controller Amanda Mackie